CREATURA - 6

70 drawings by Joan Worth

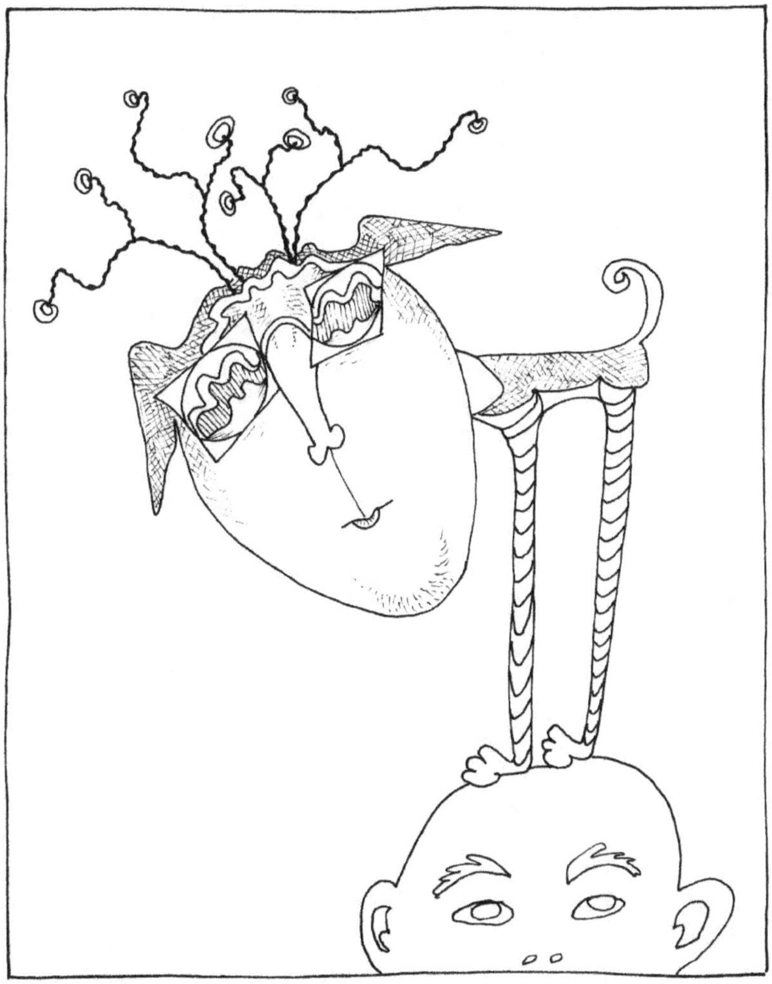

De Pere, Wisconsin
ISBN: 978-1798652350

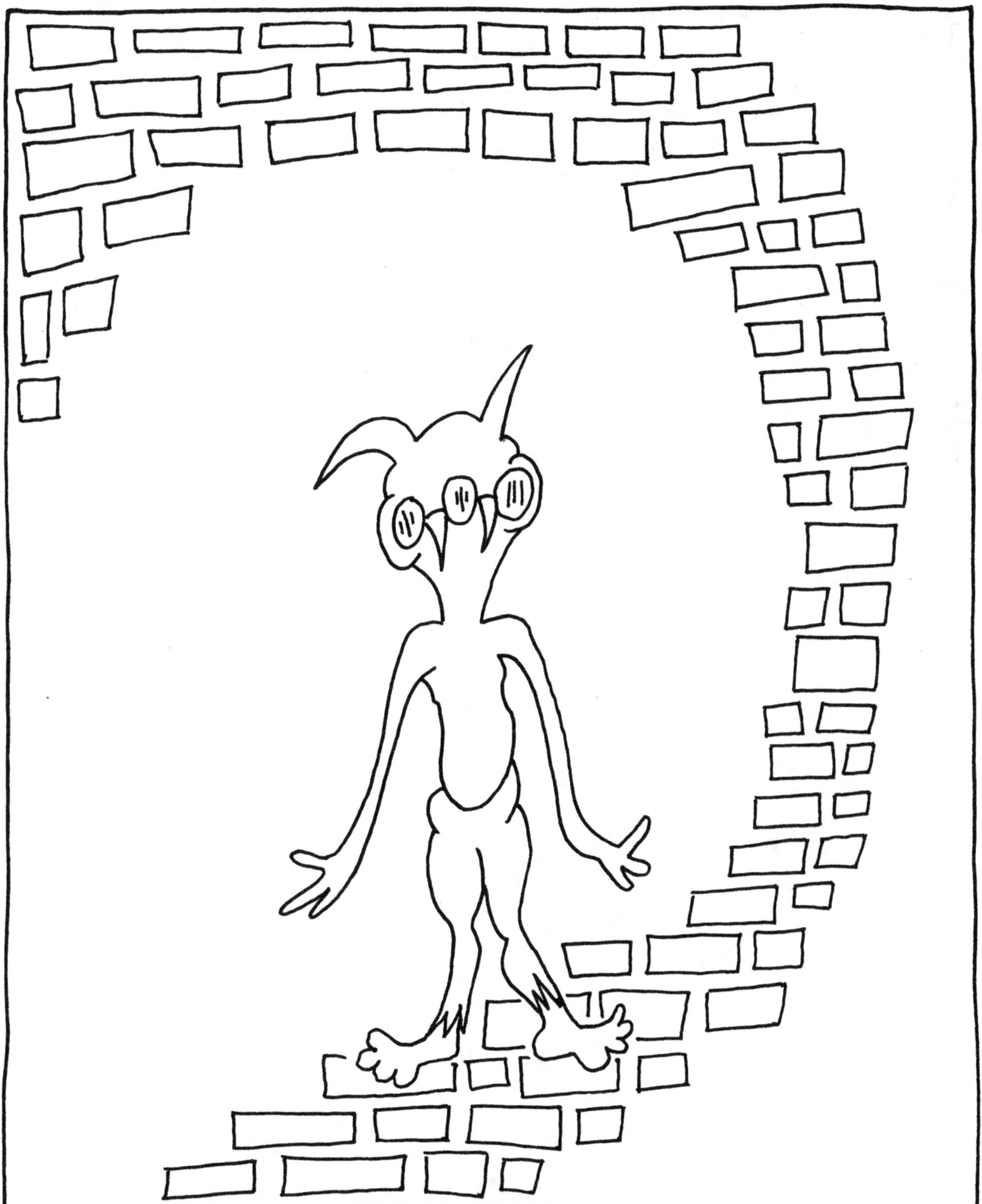

CREATURA #6

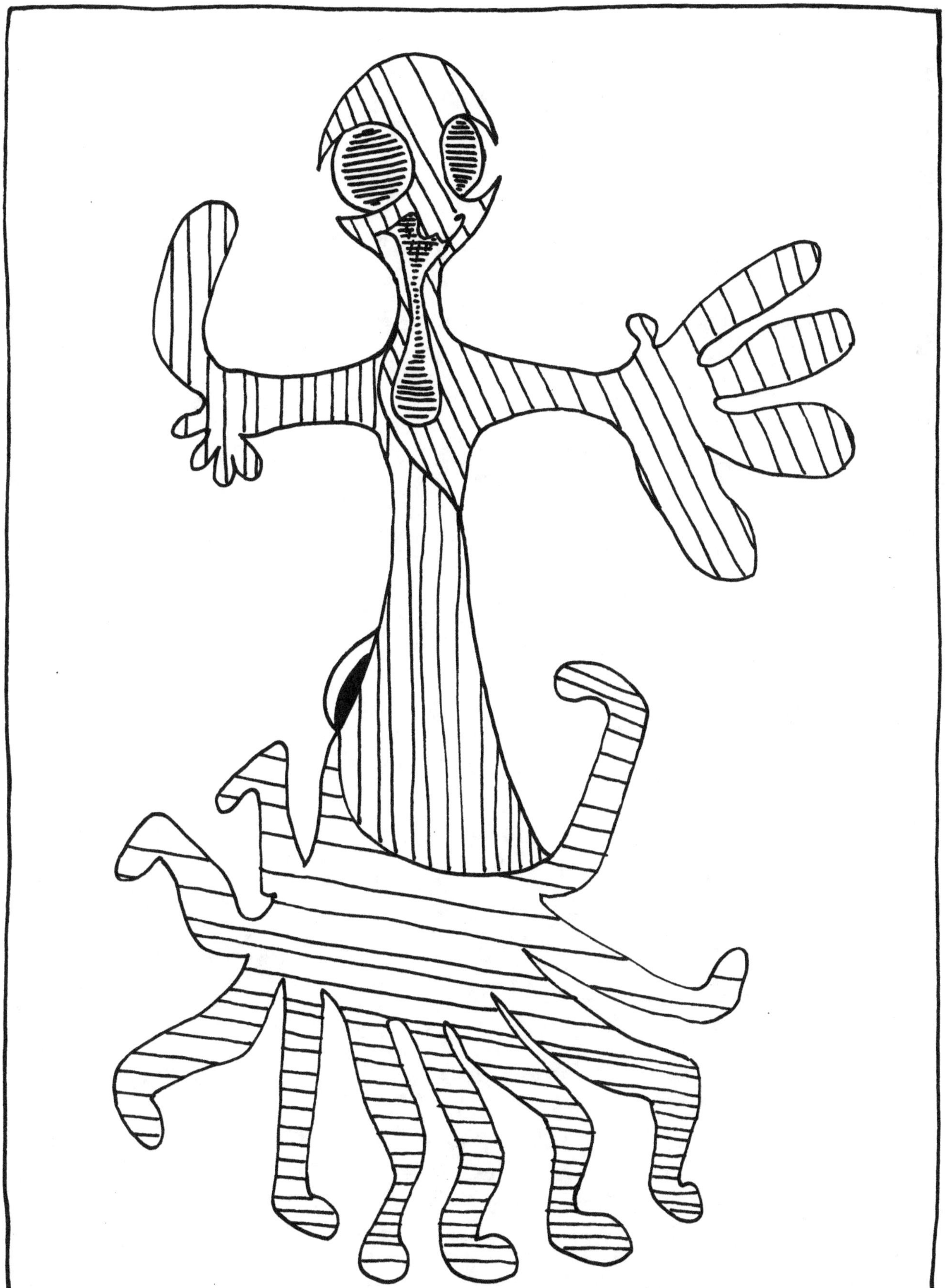

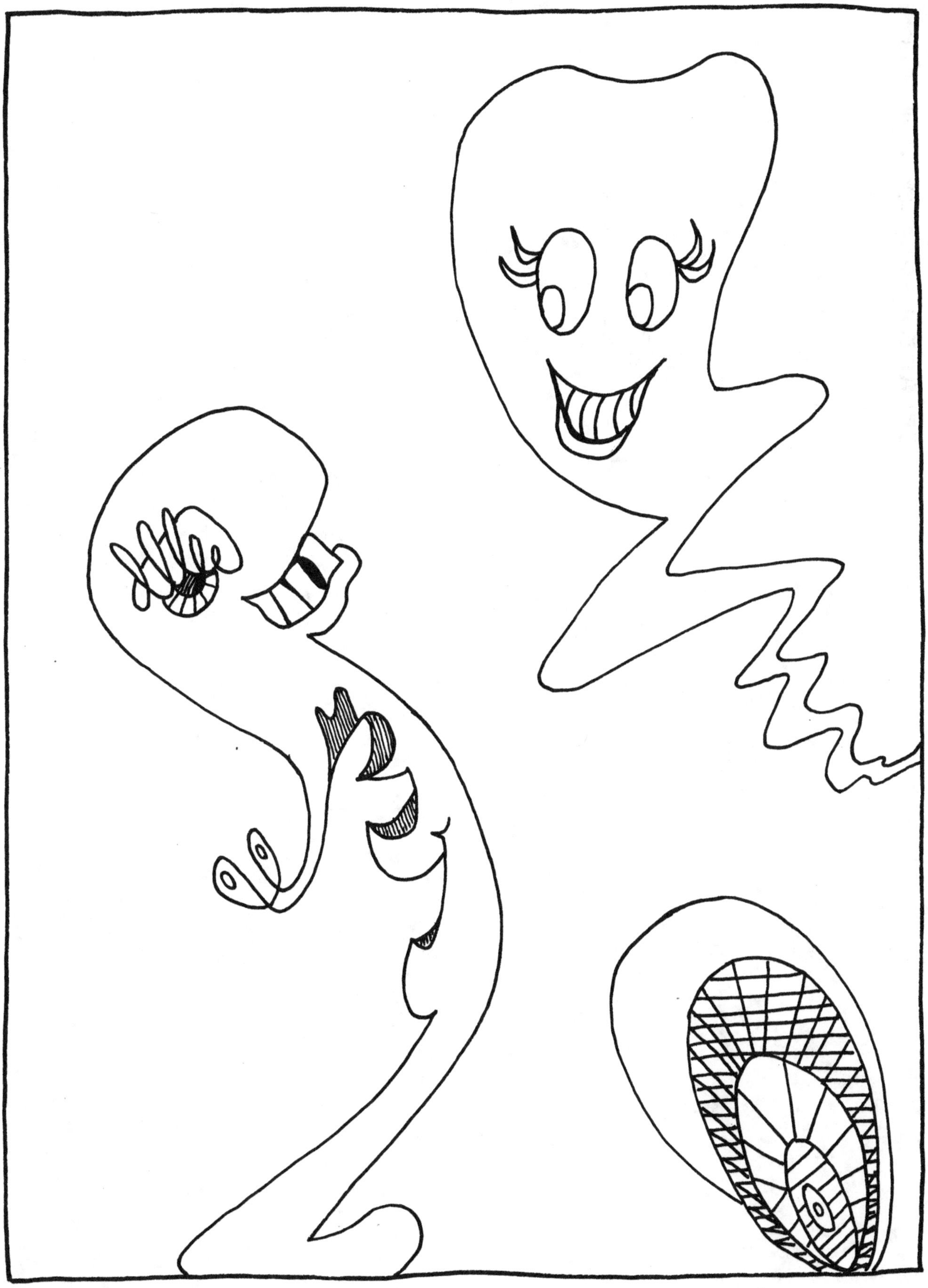

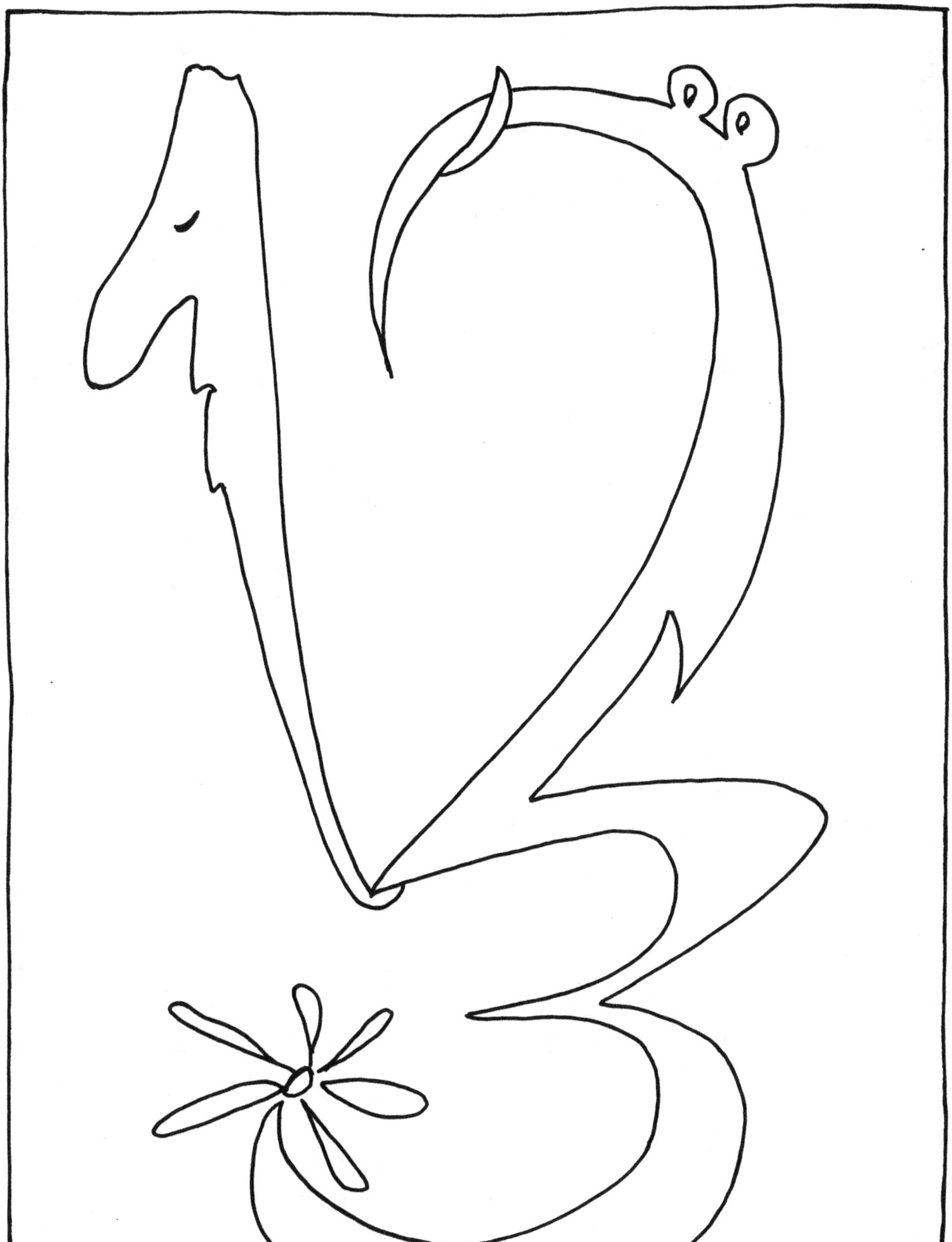

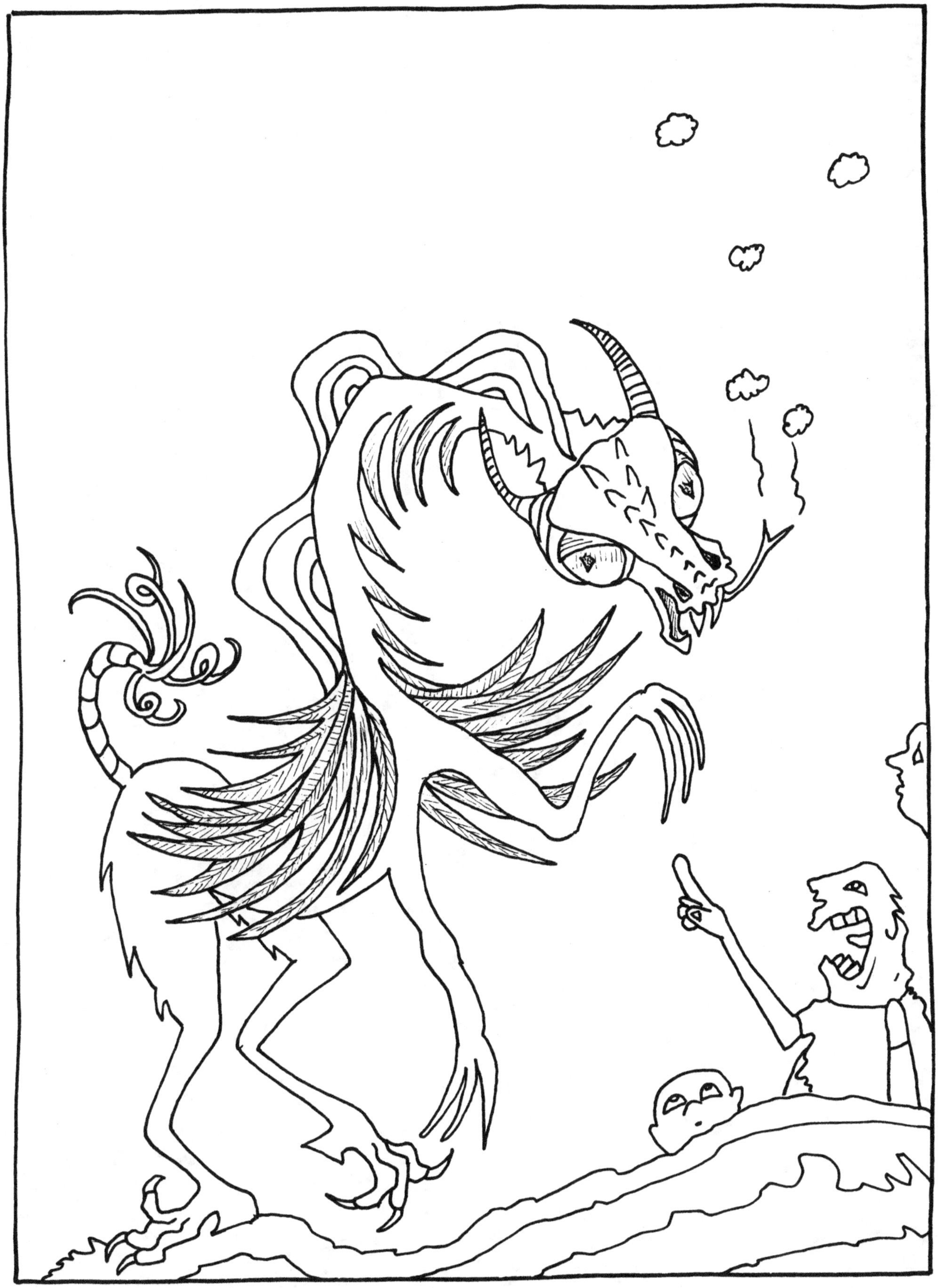

CREATURA #6

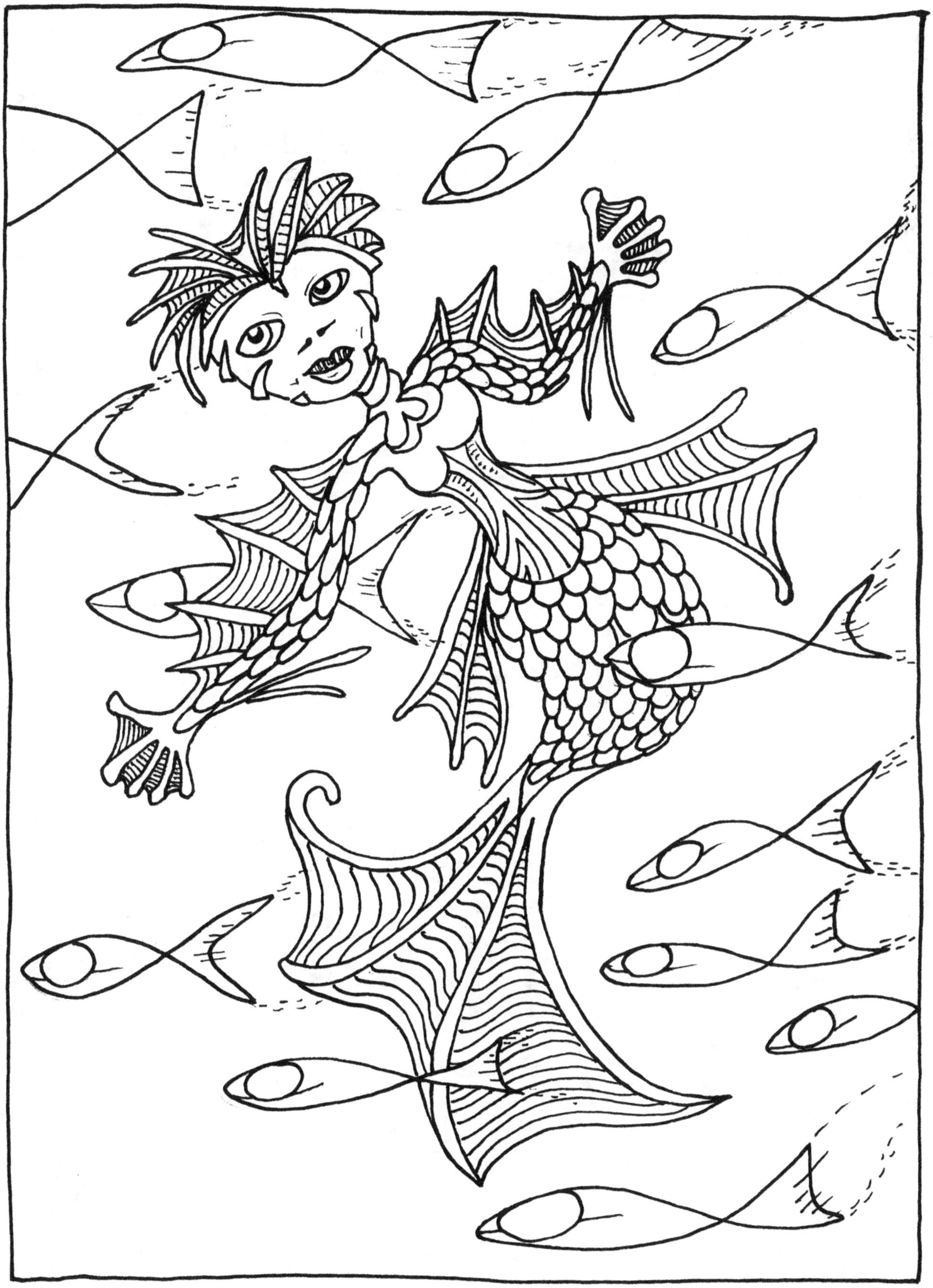

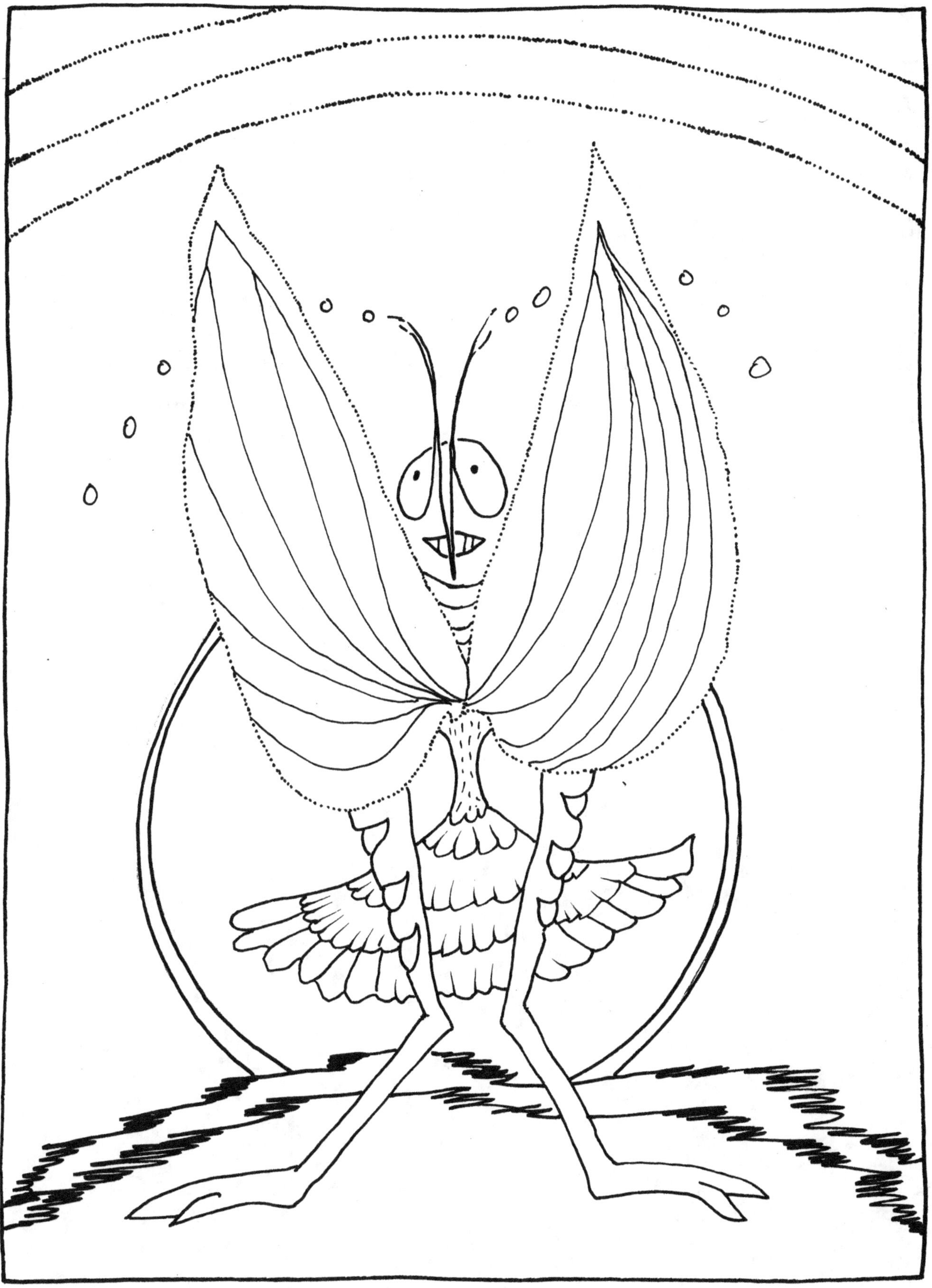

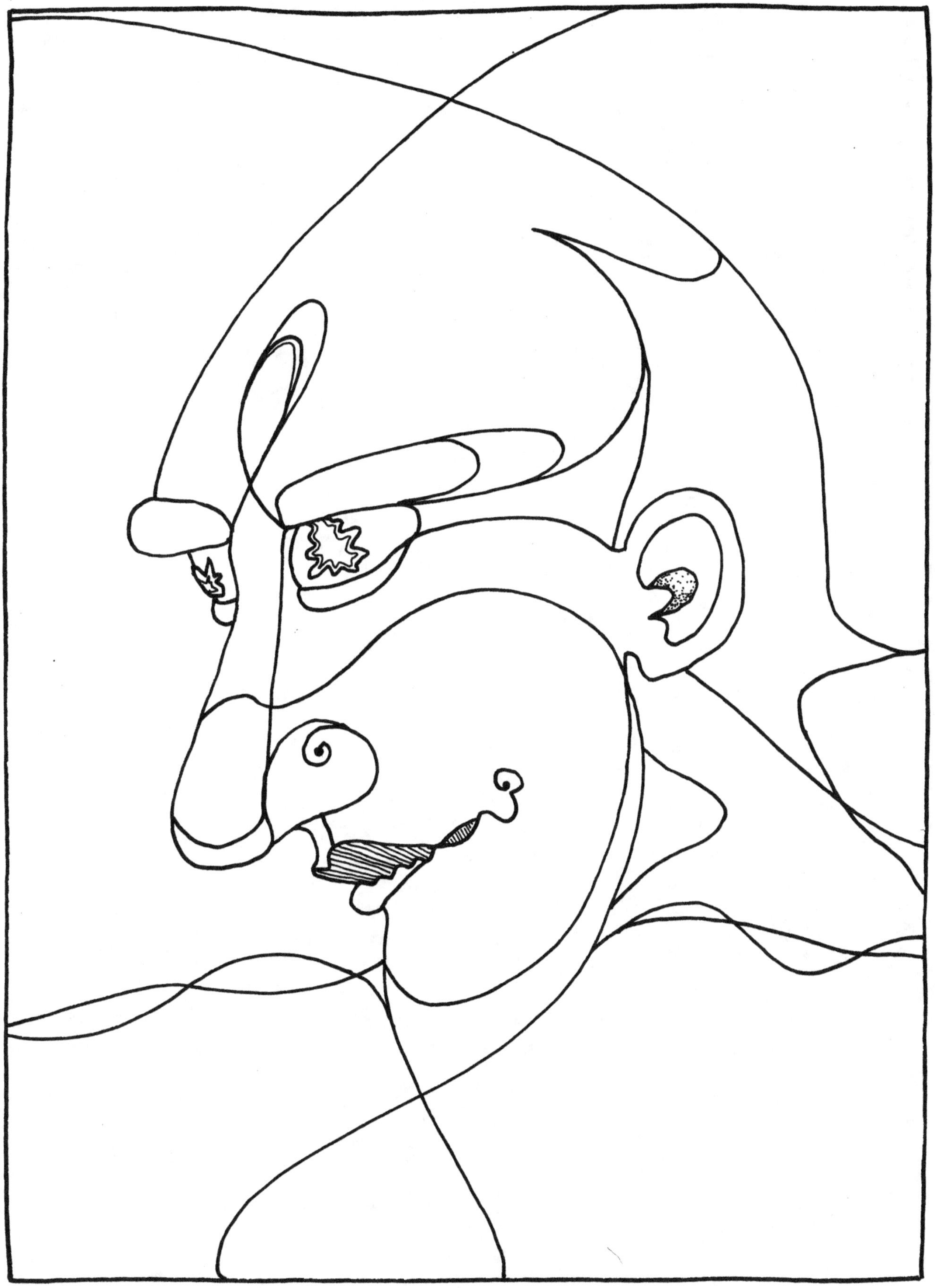

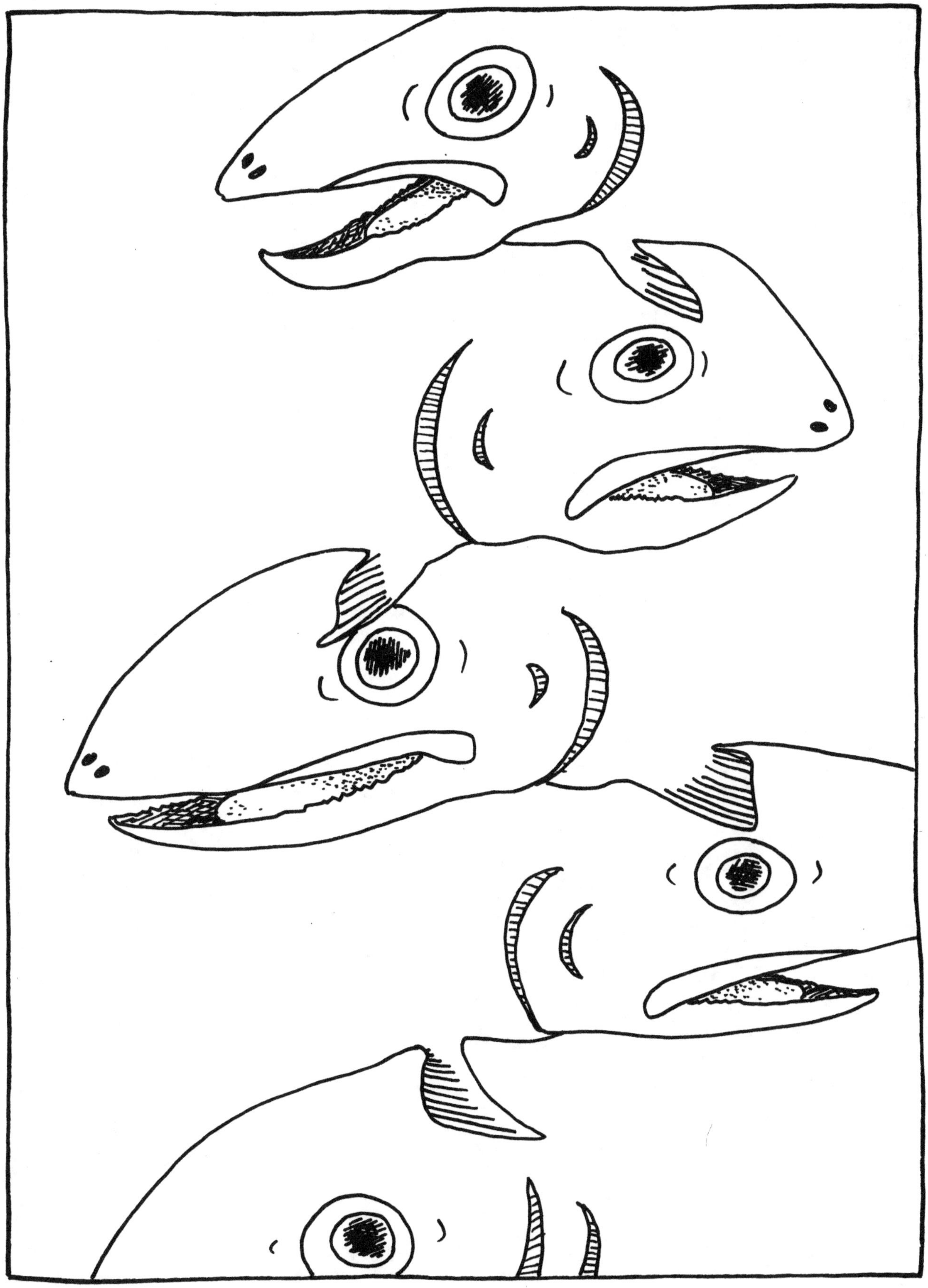

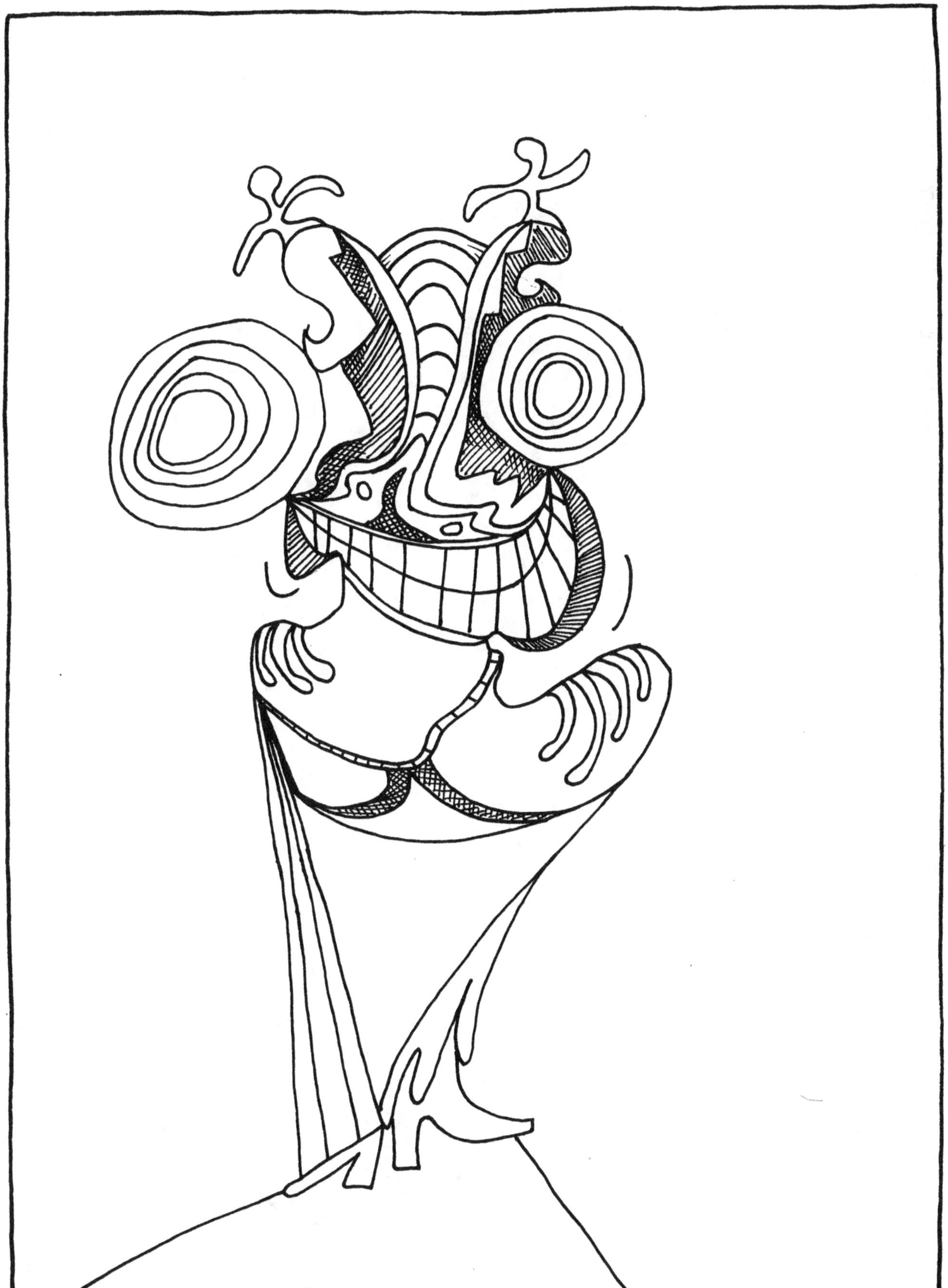

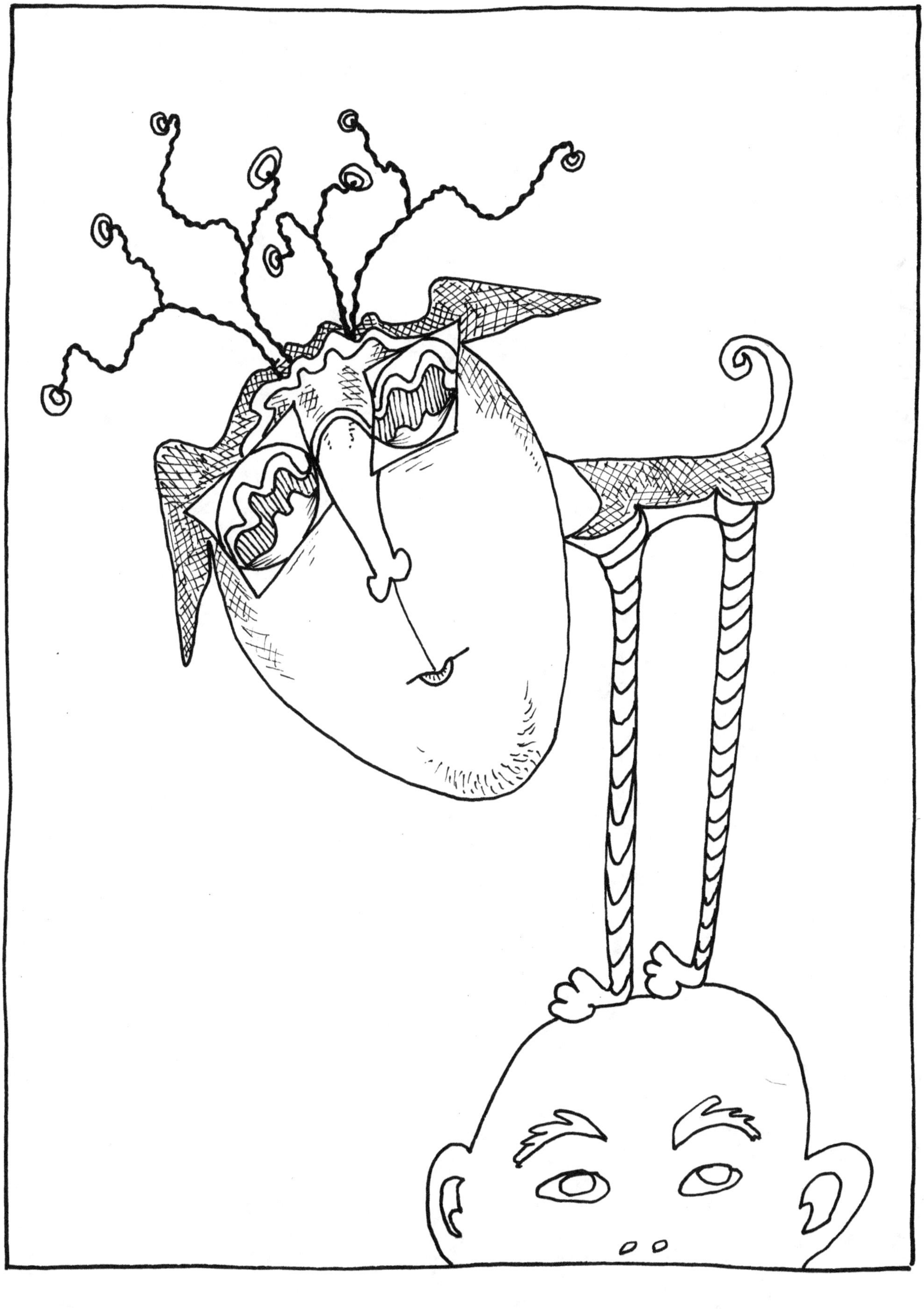

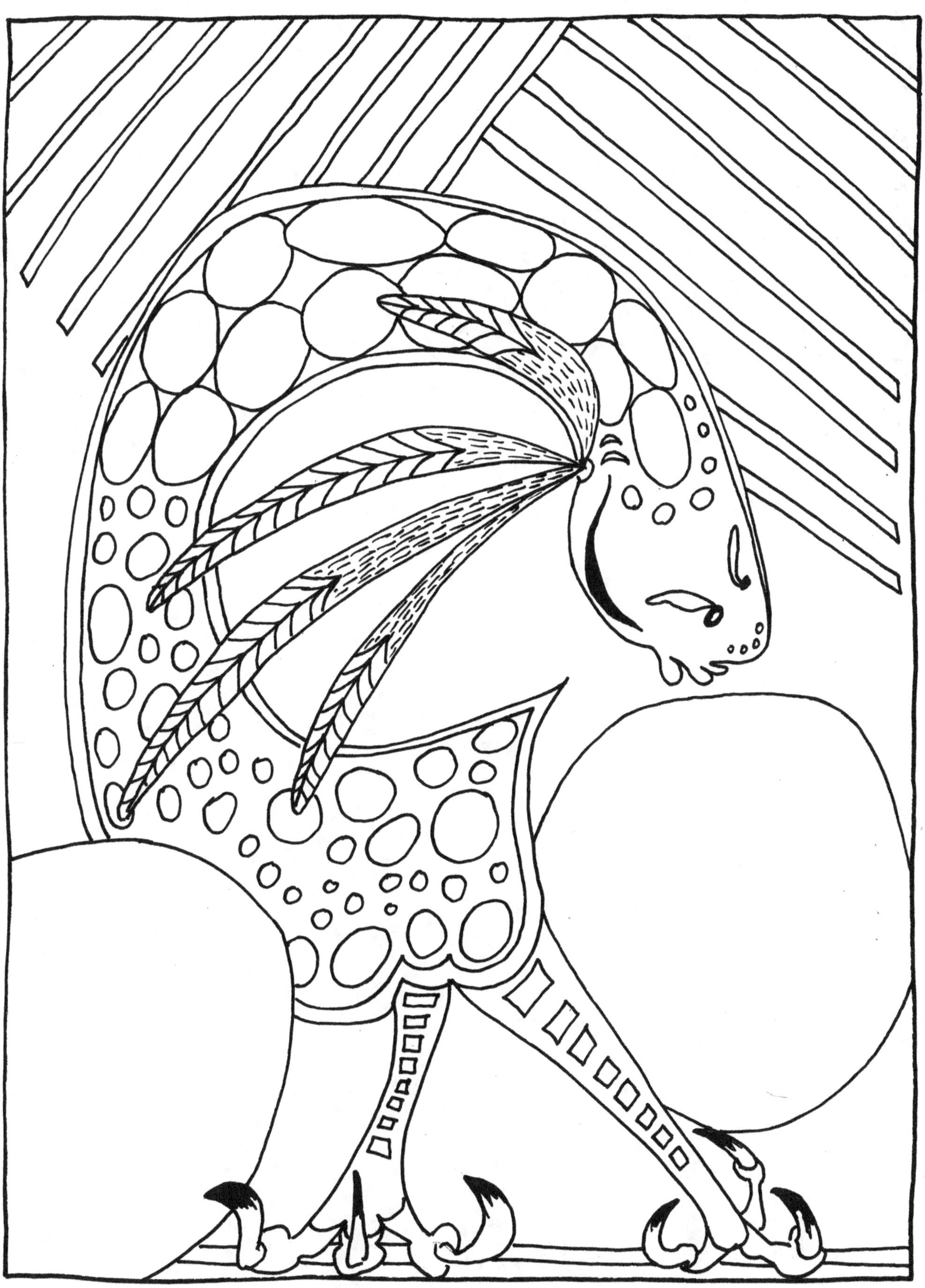

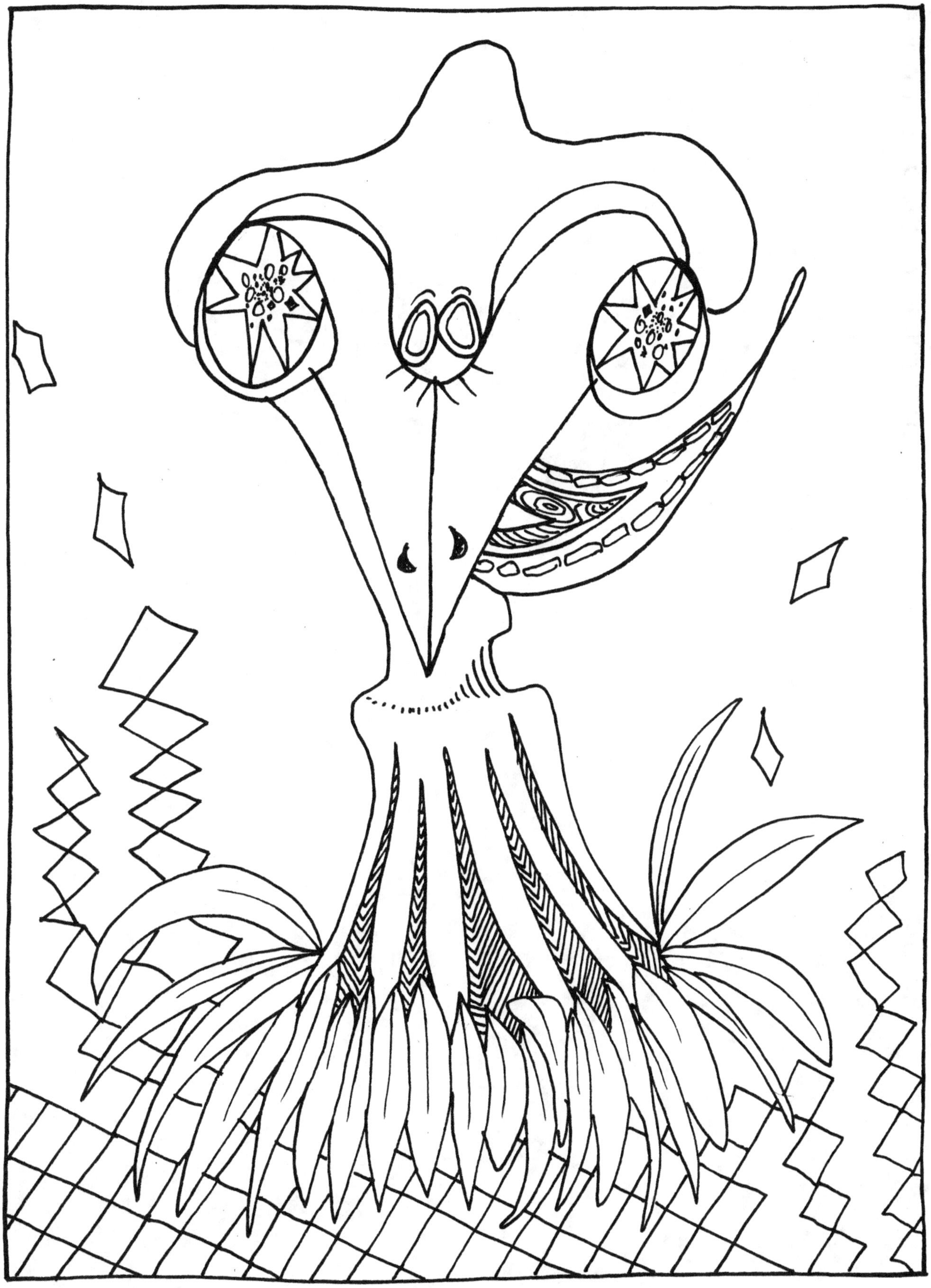

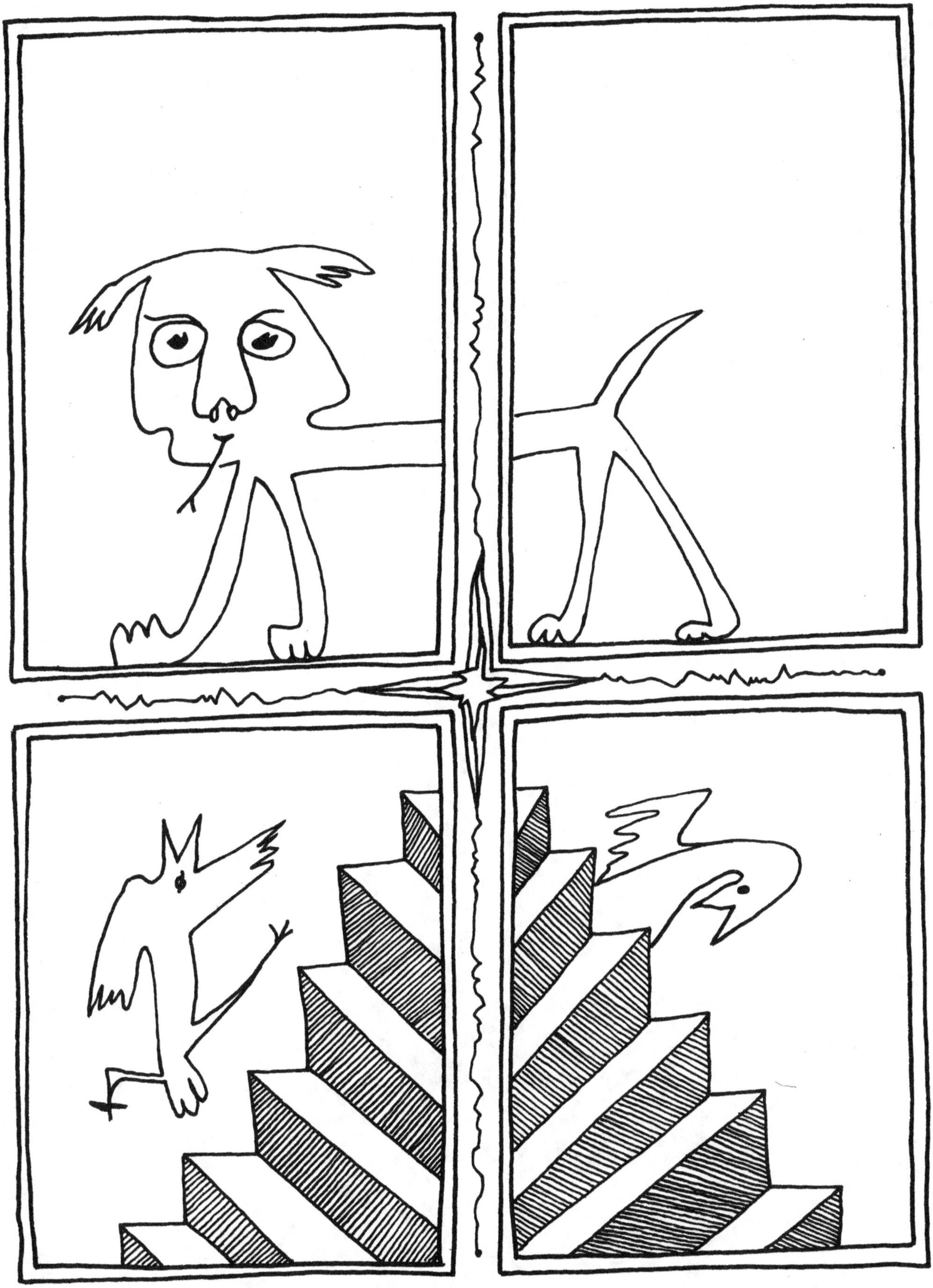

CREATURA #6

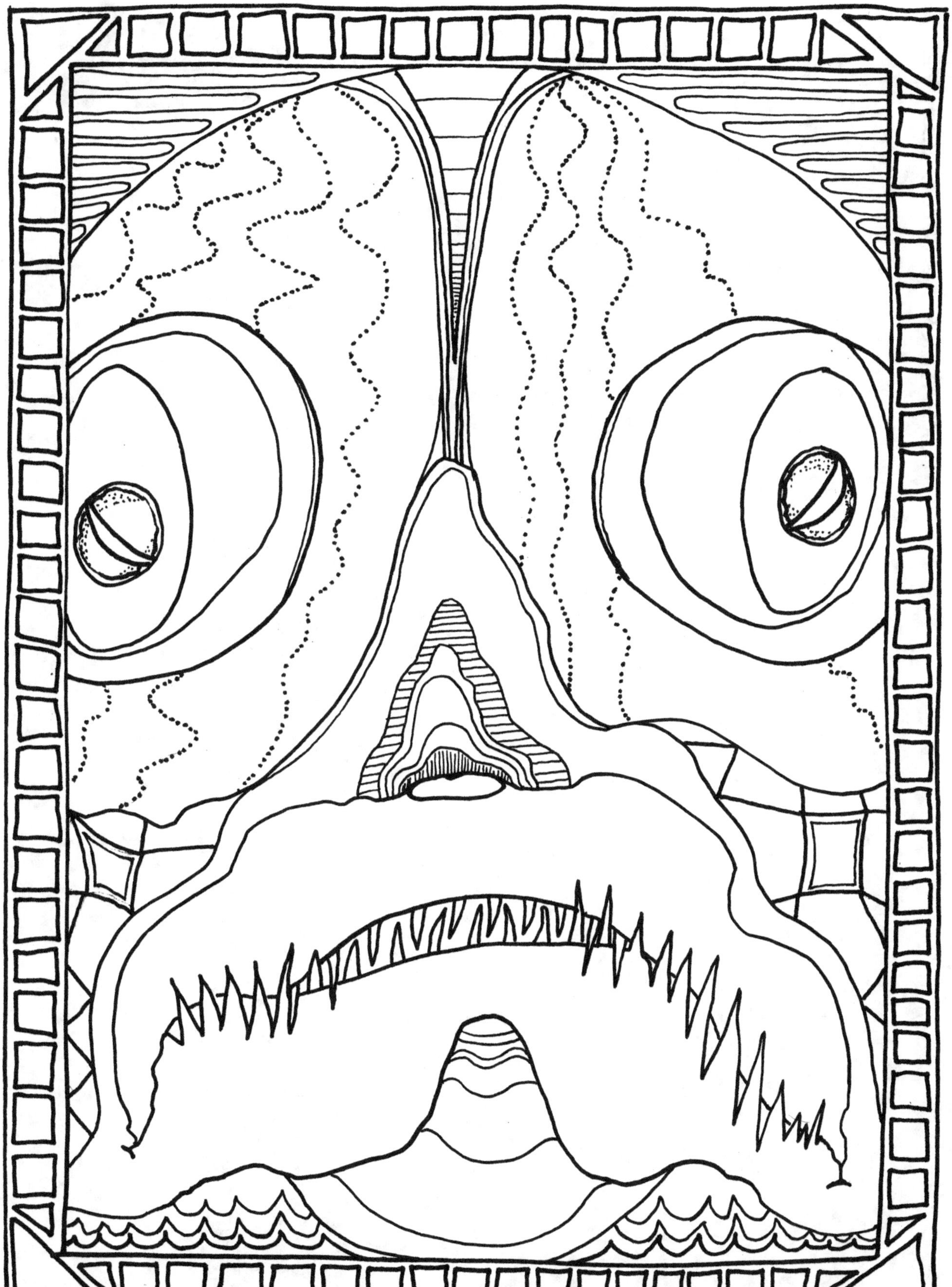

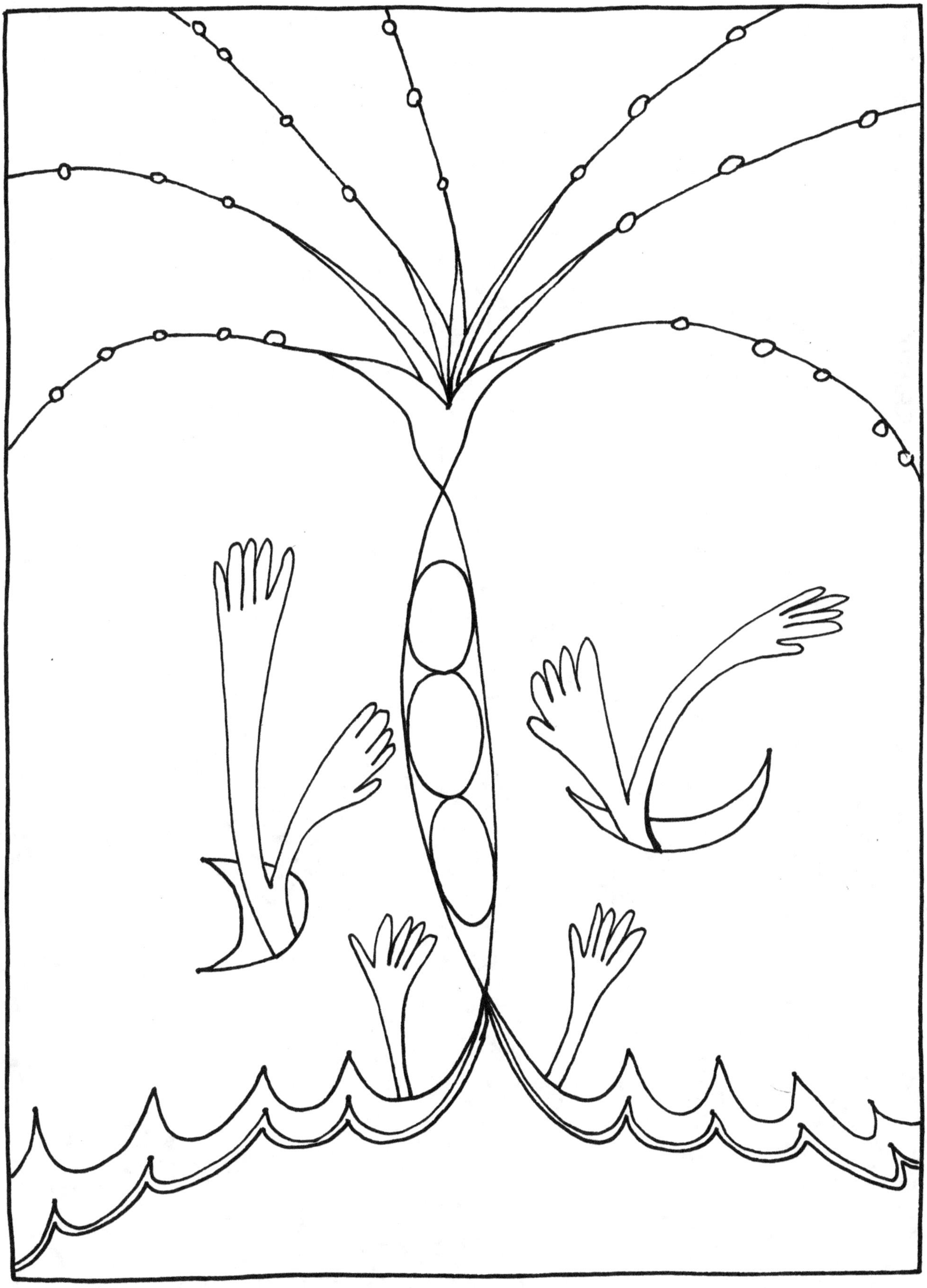

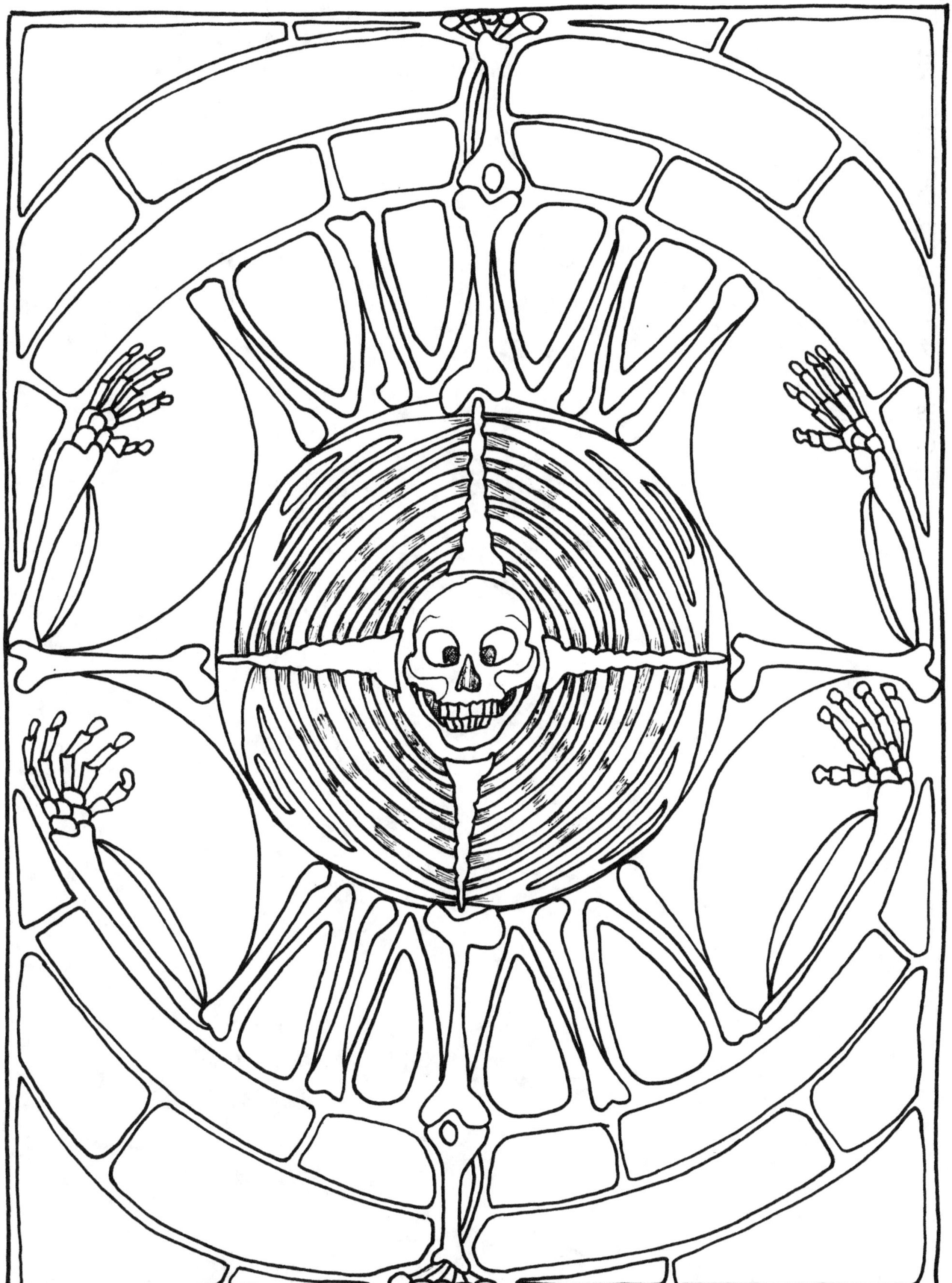

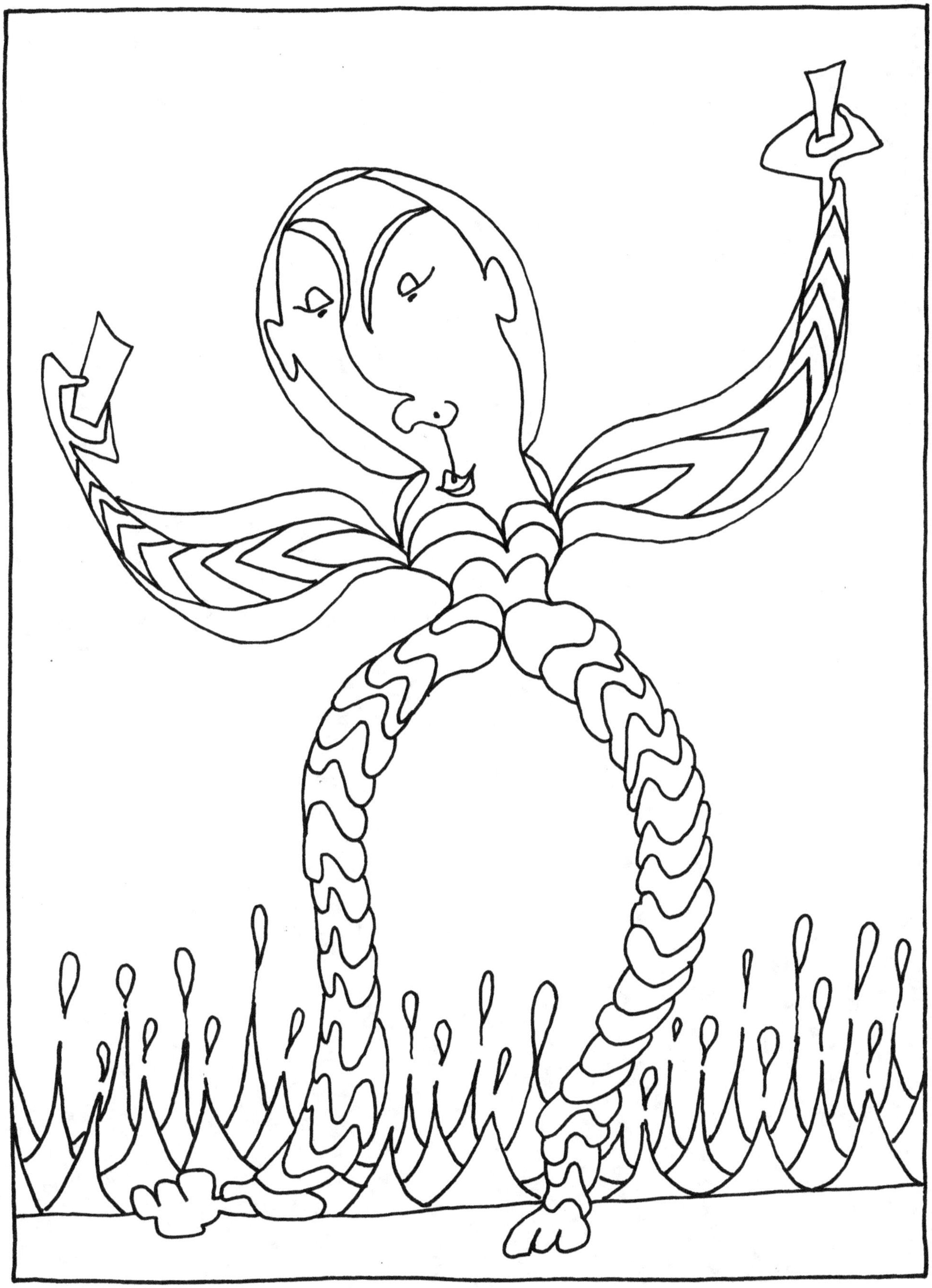

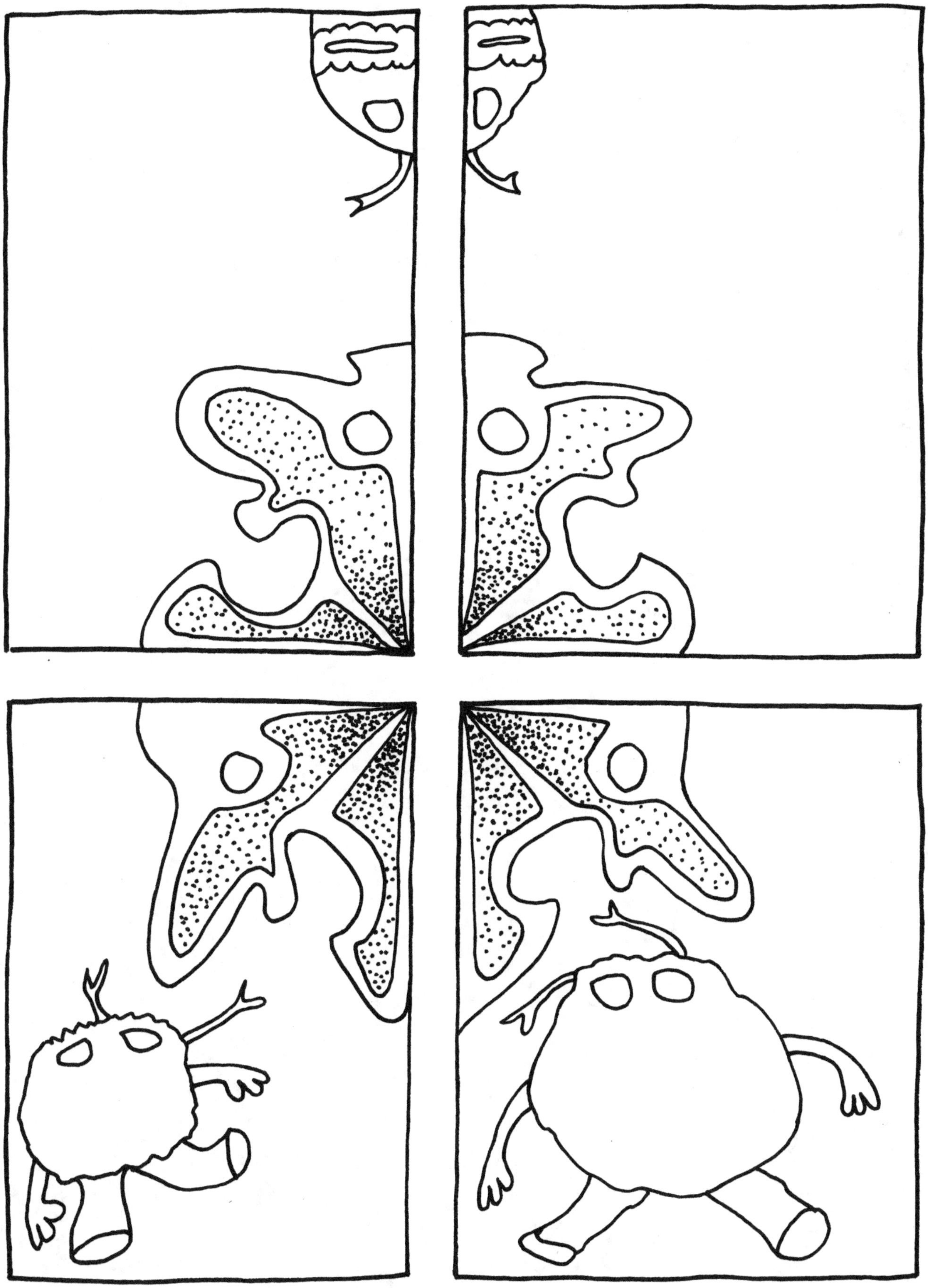

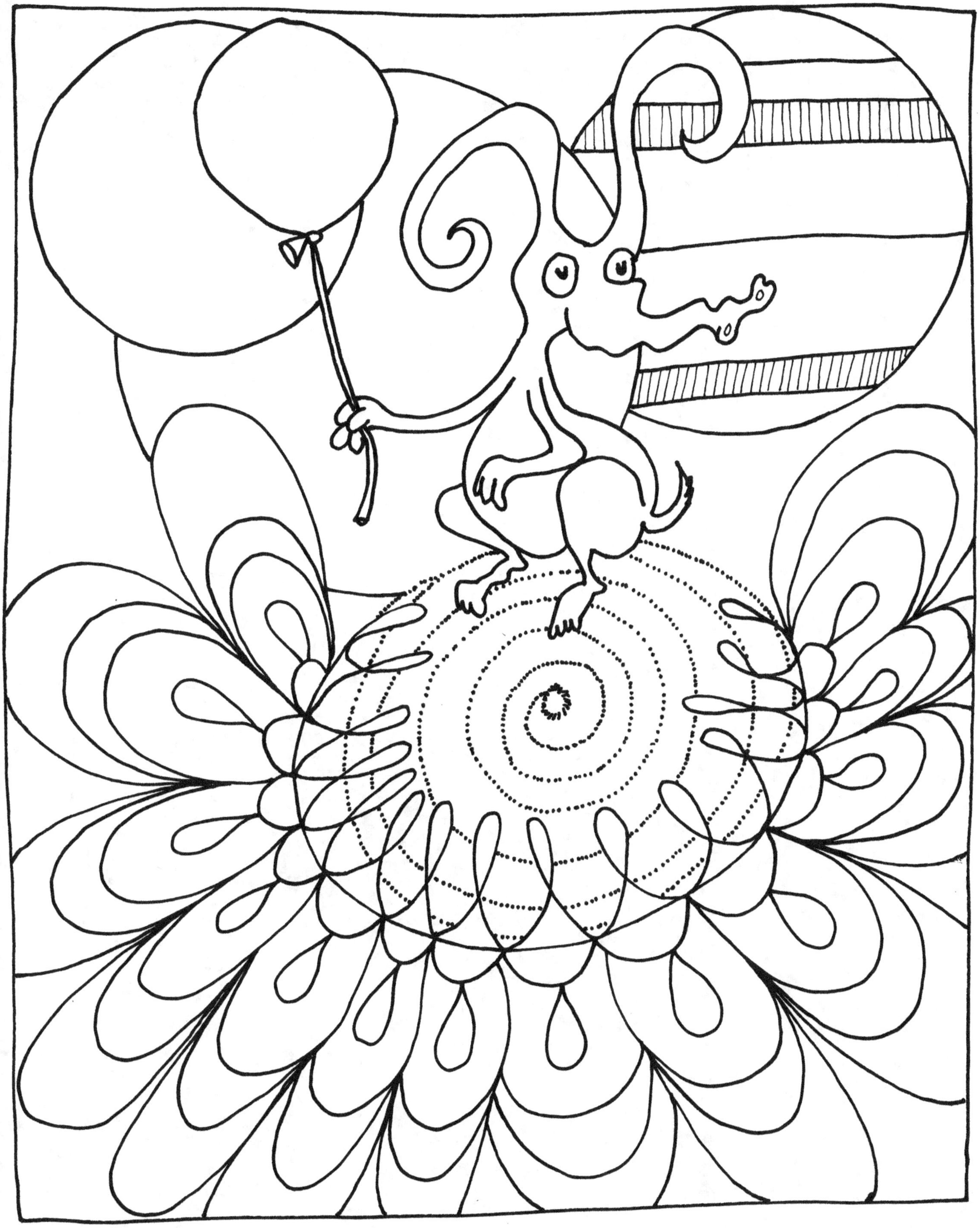

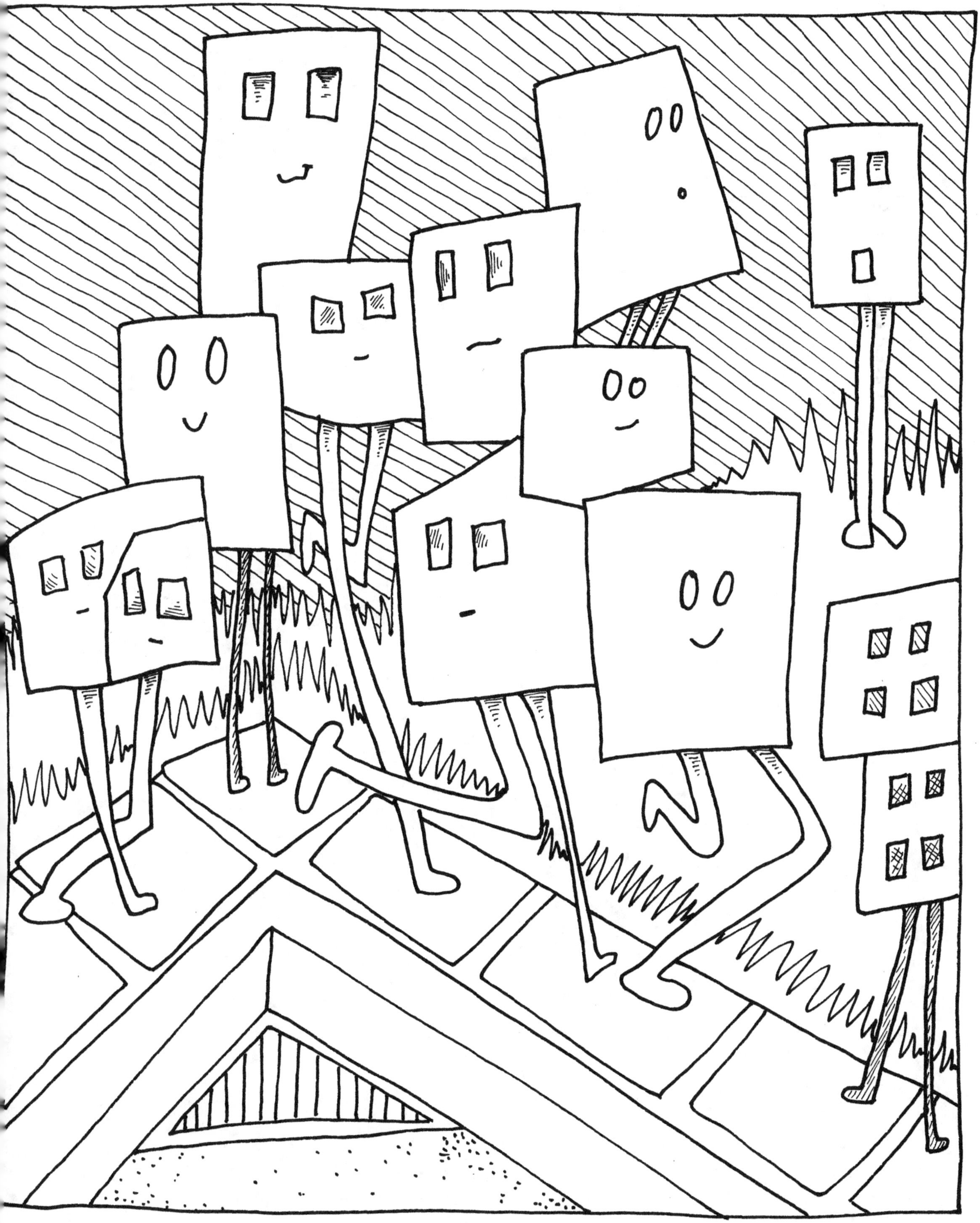

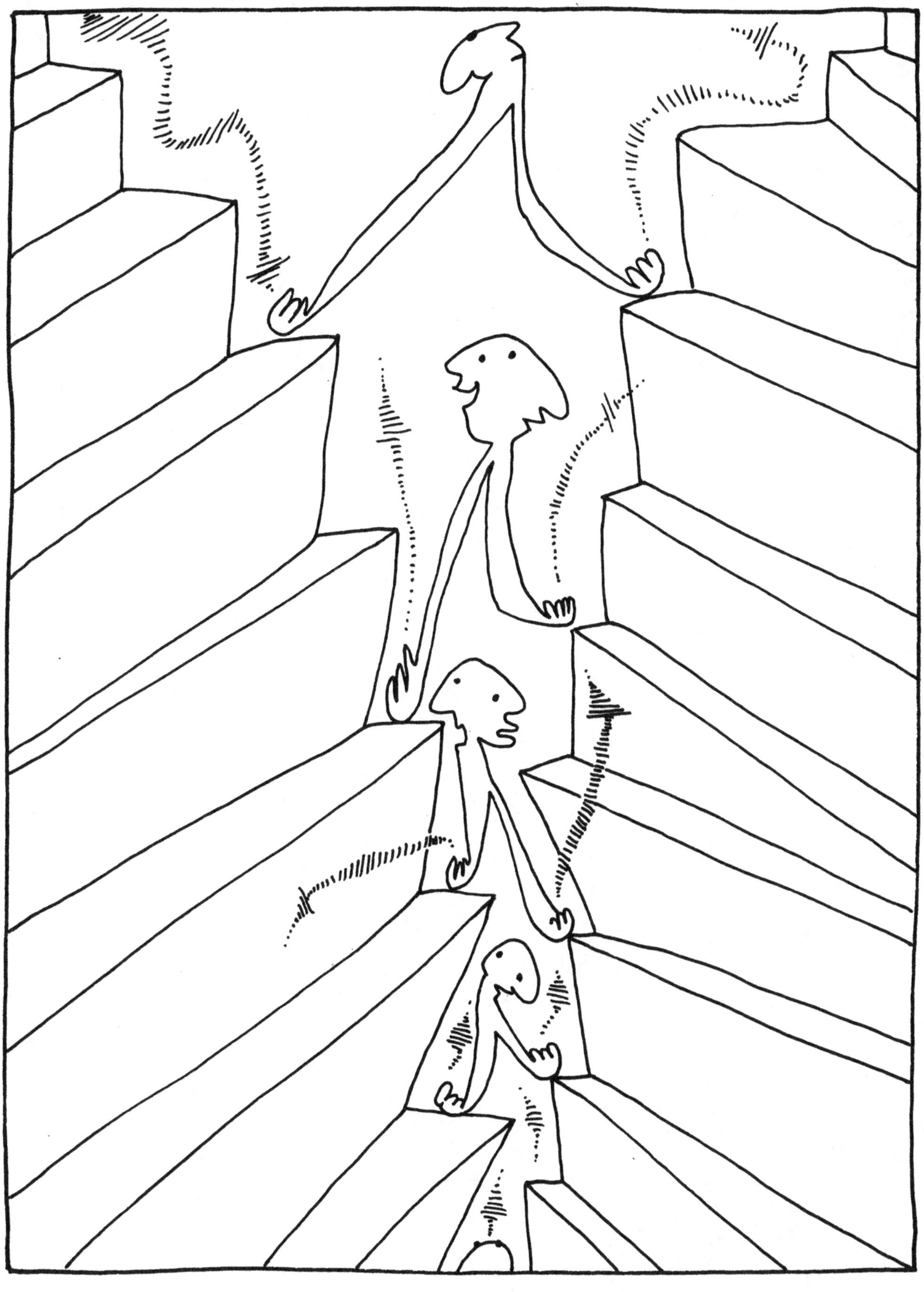

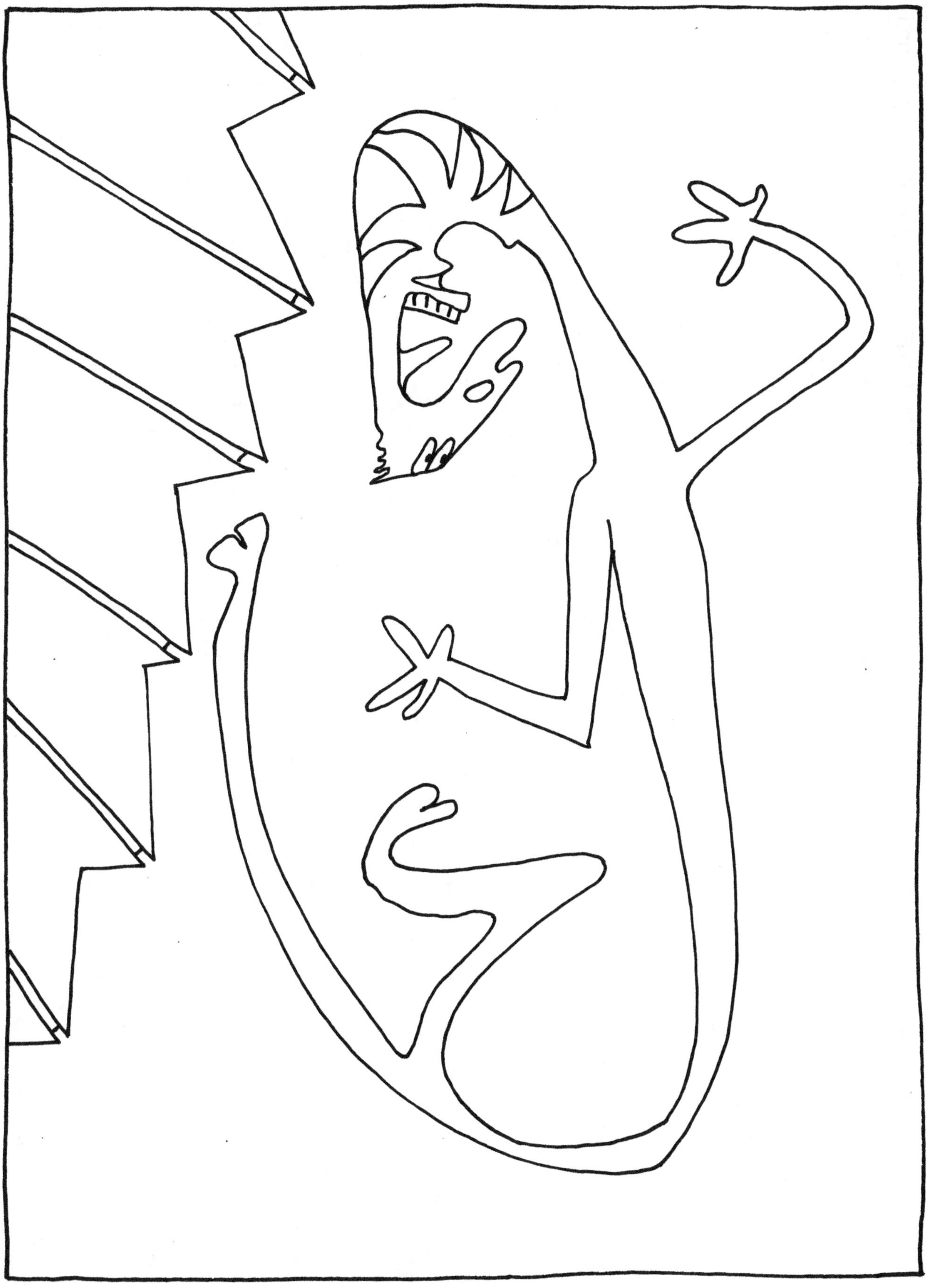

CREATURA #6

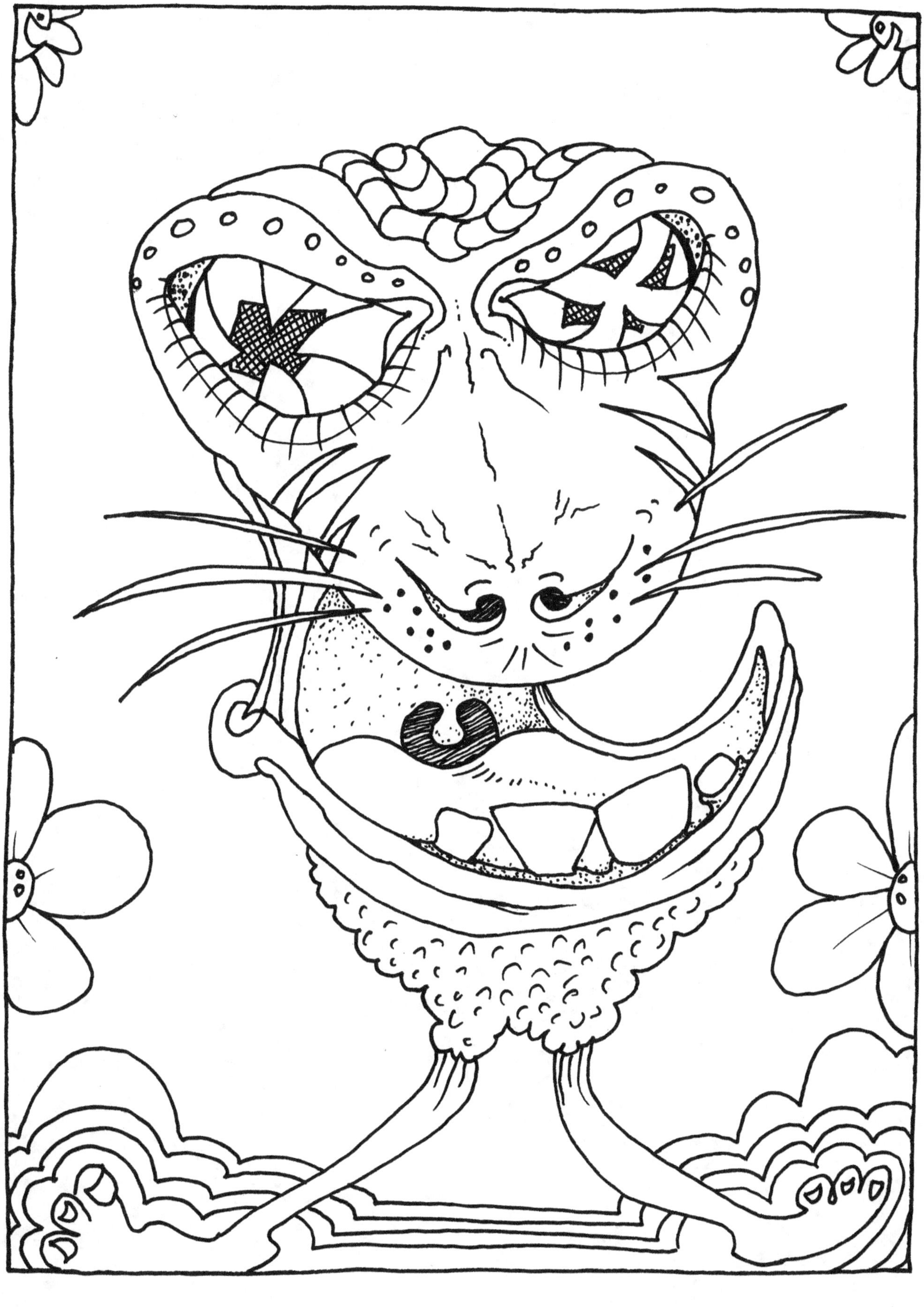

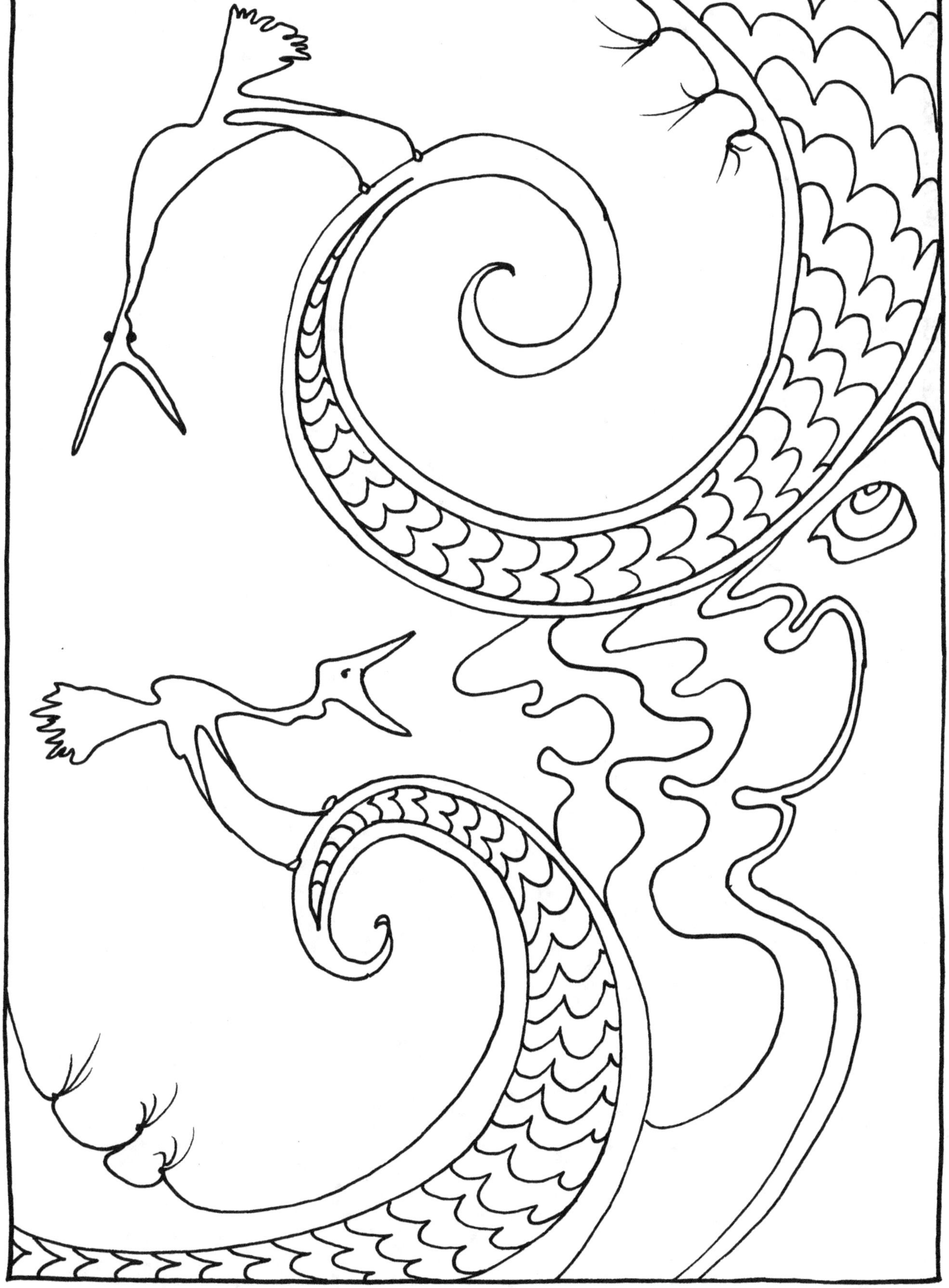

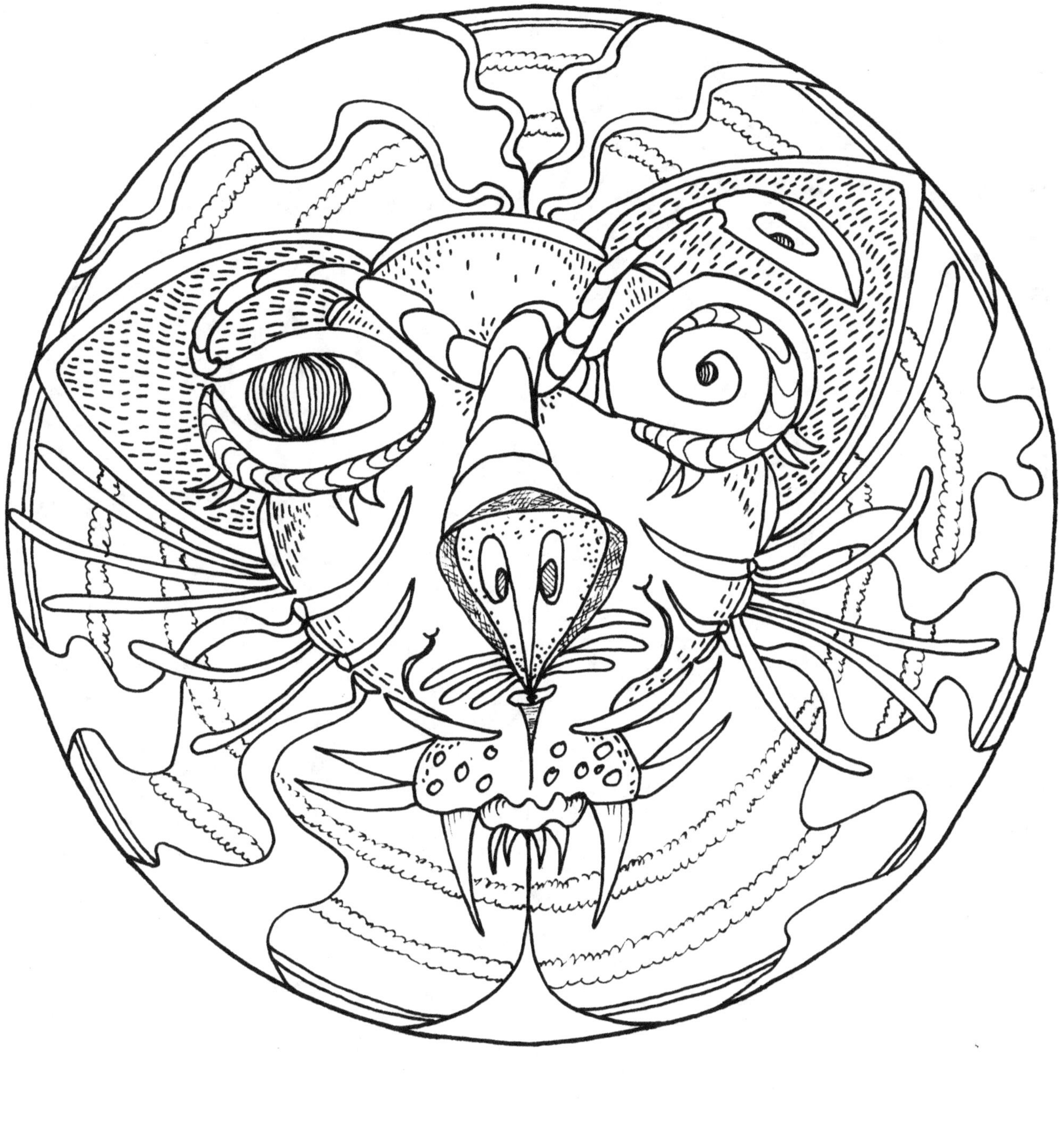

CREATURA #6 ©2019 Joan Worth

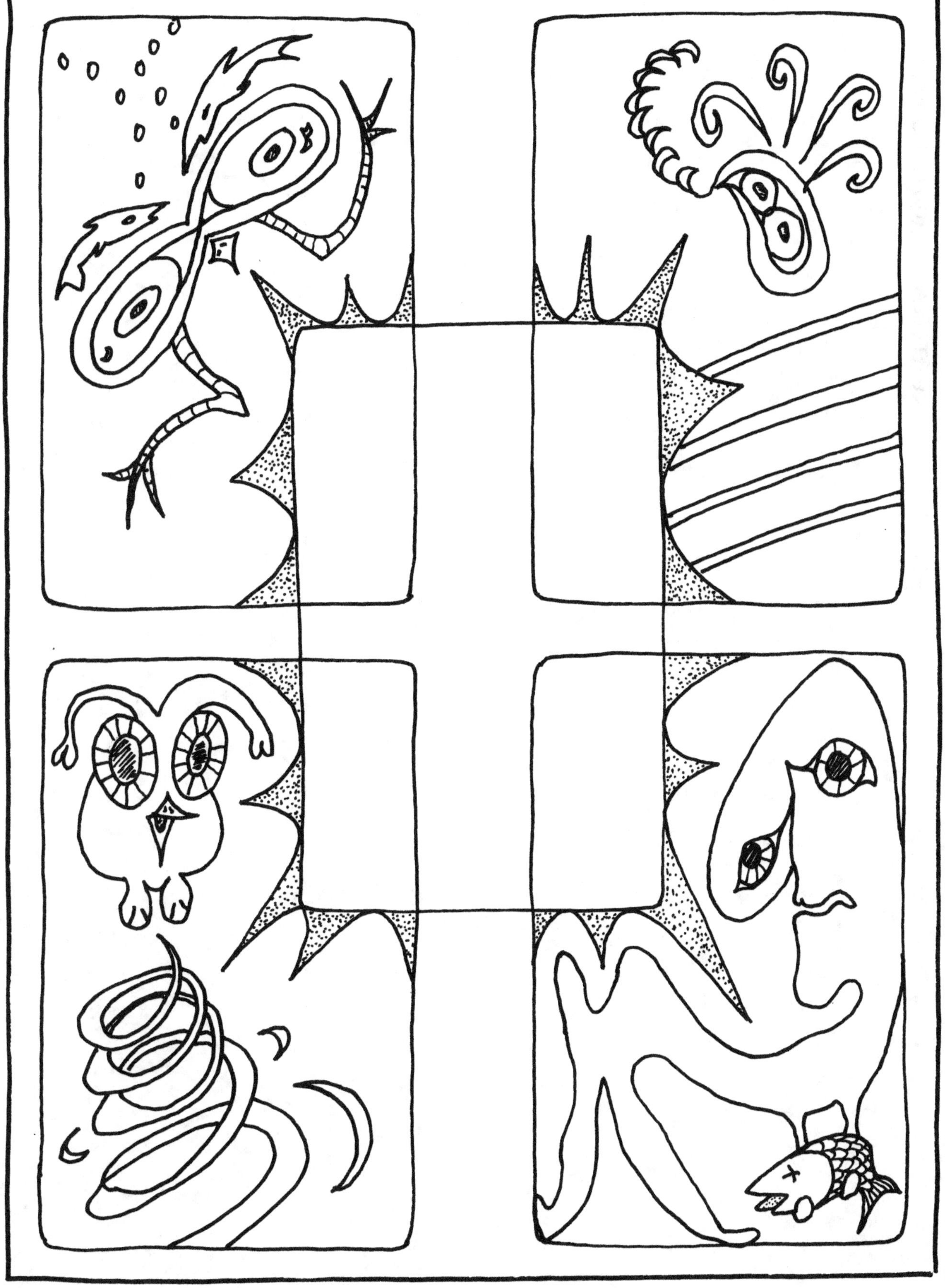

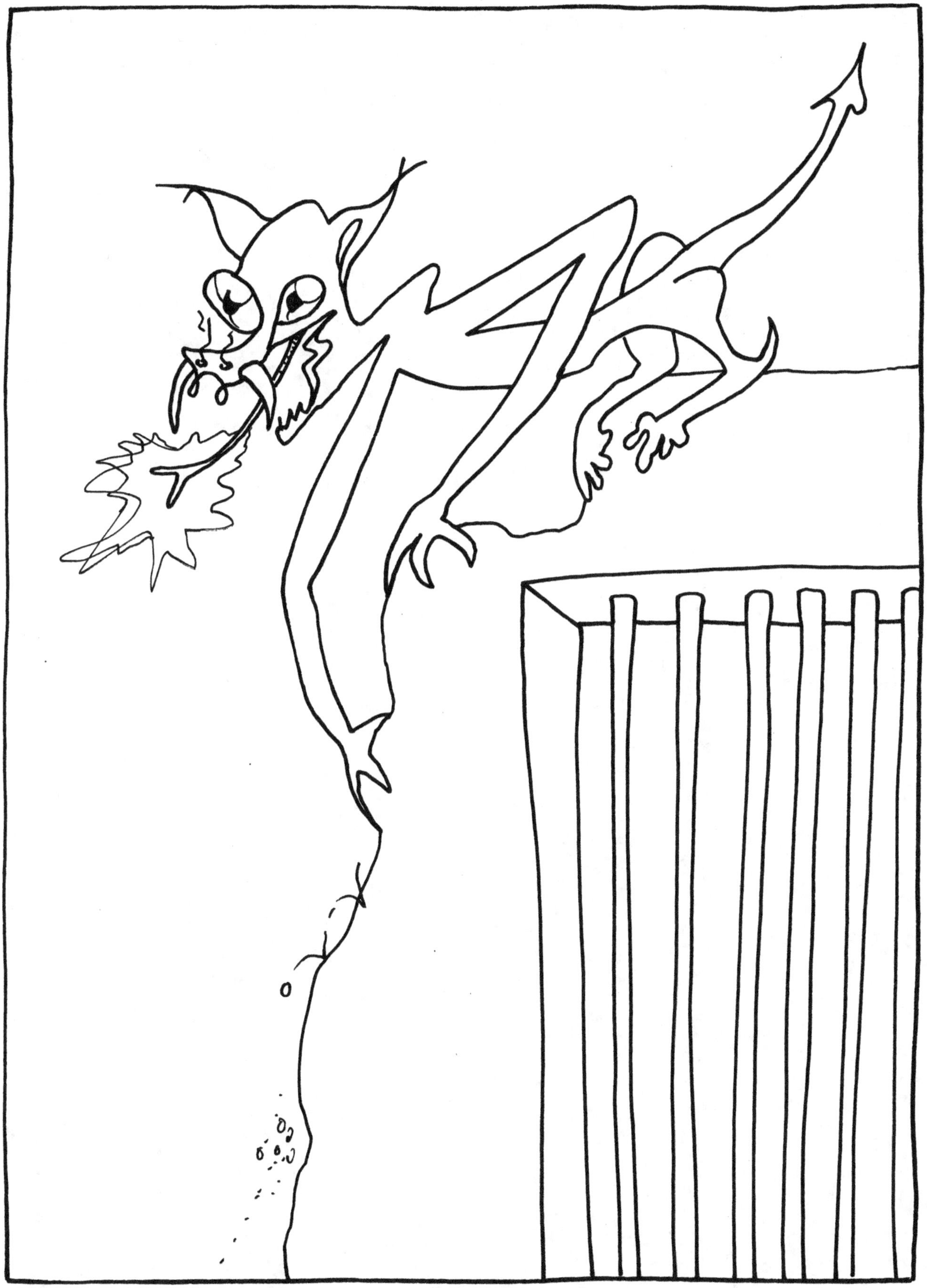

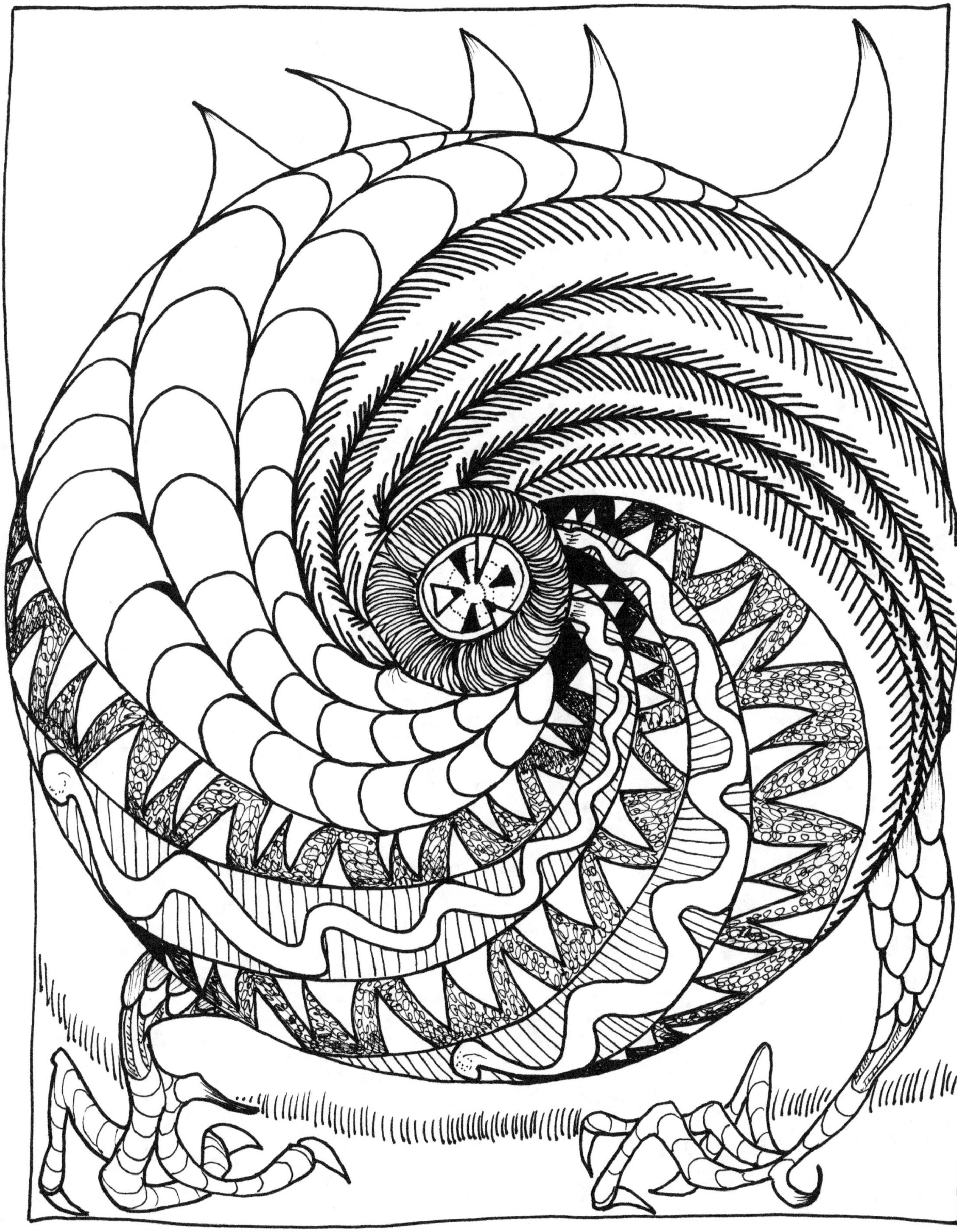

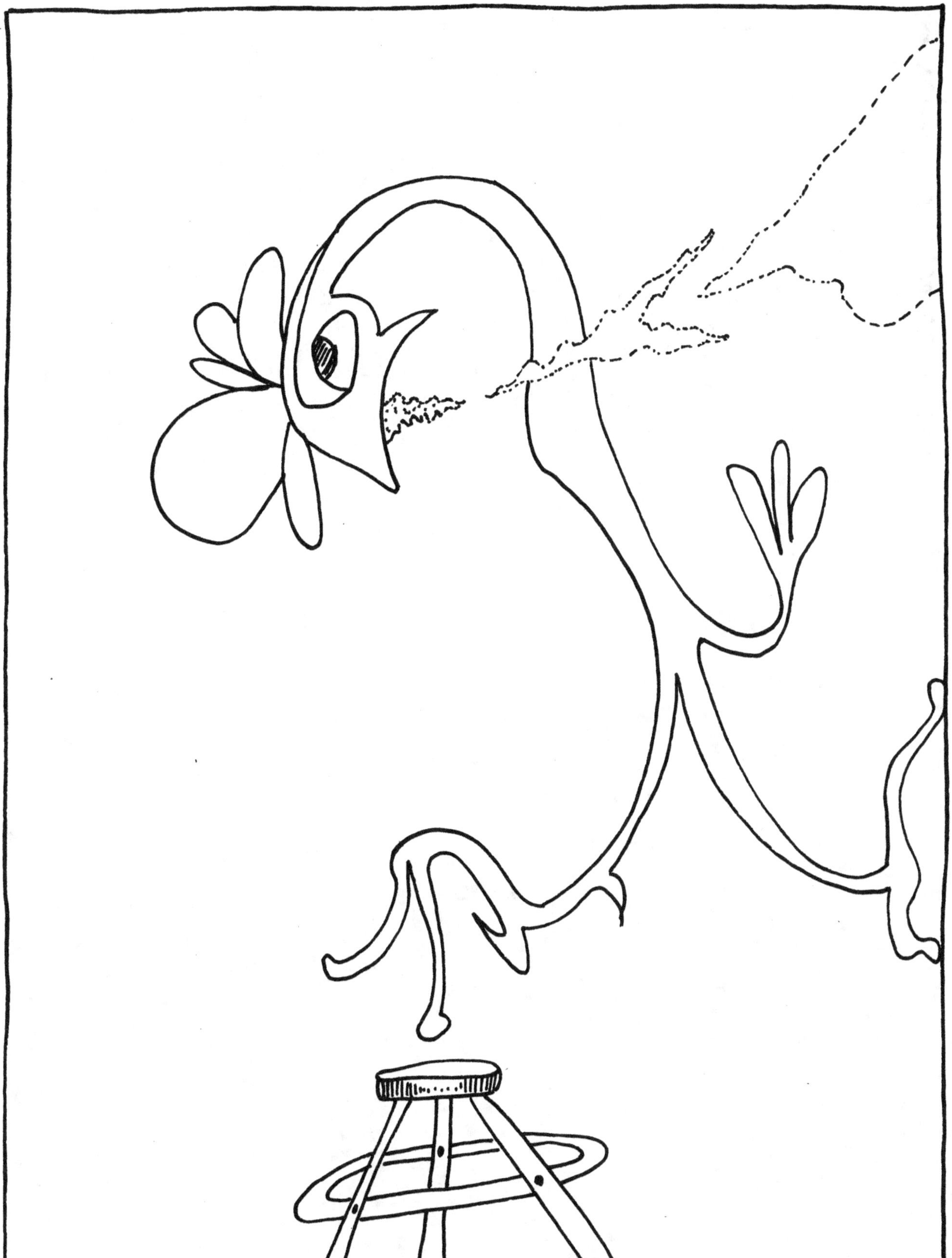

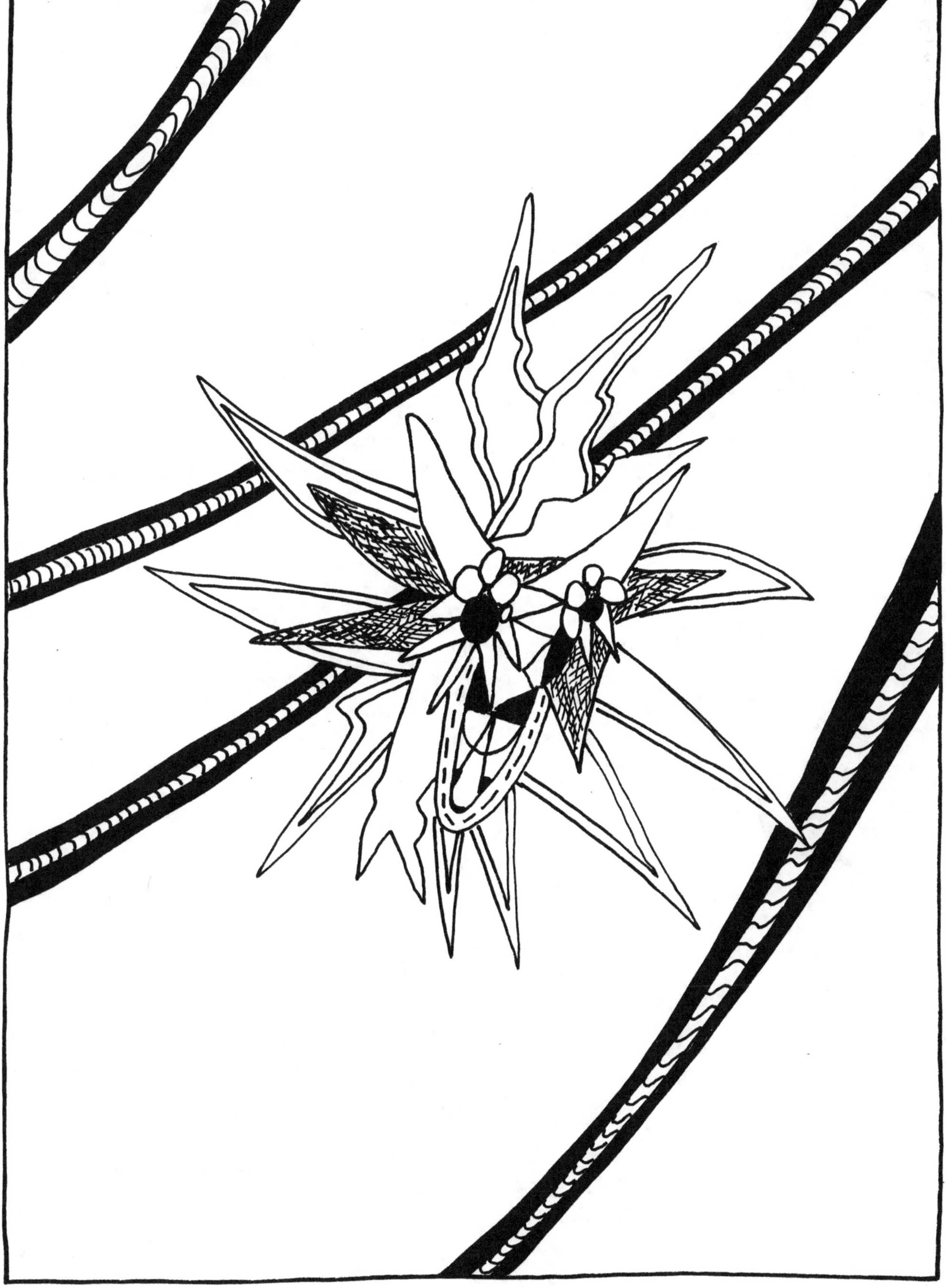

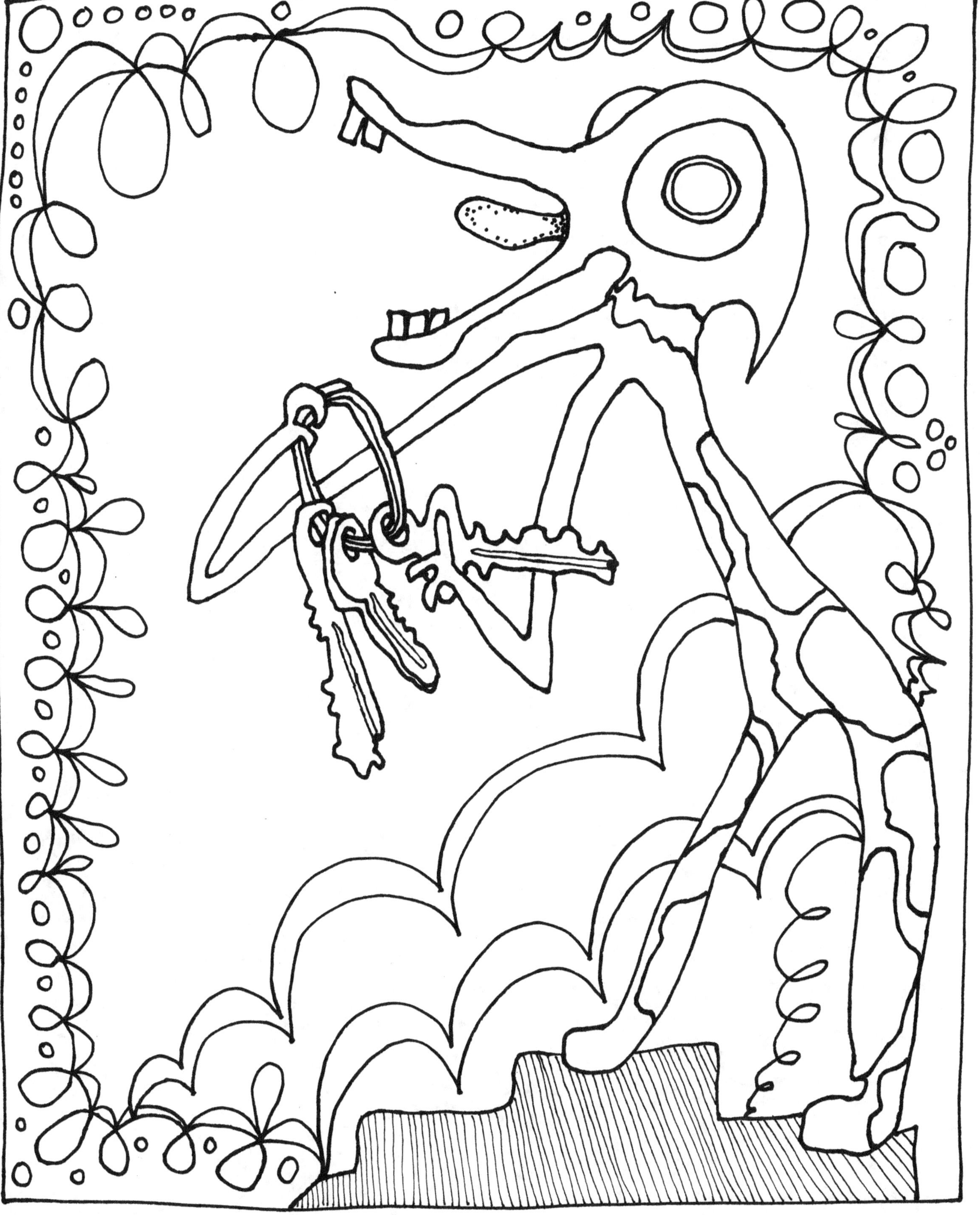

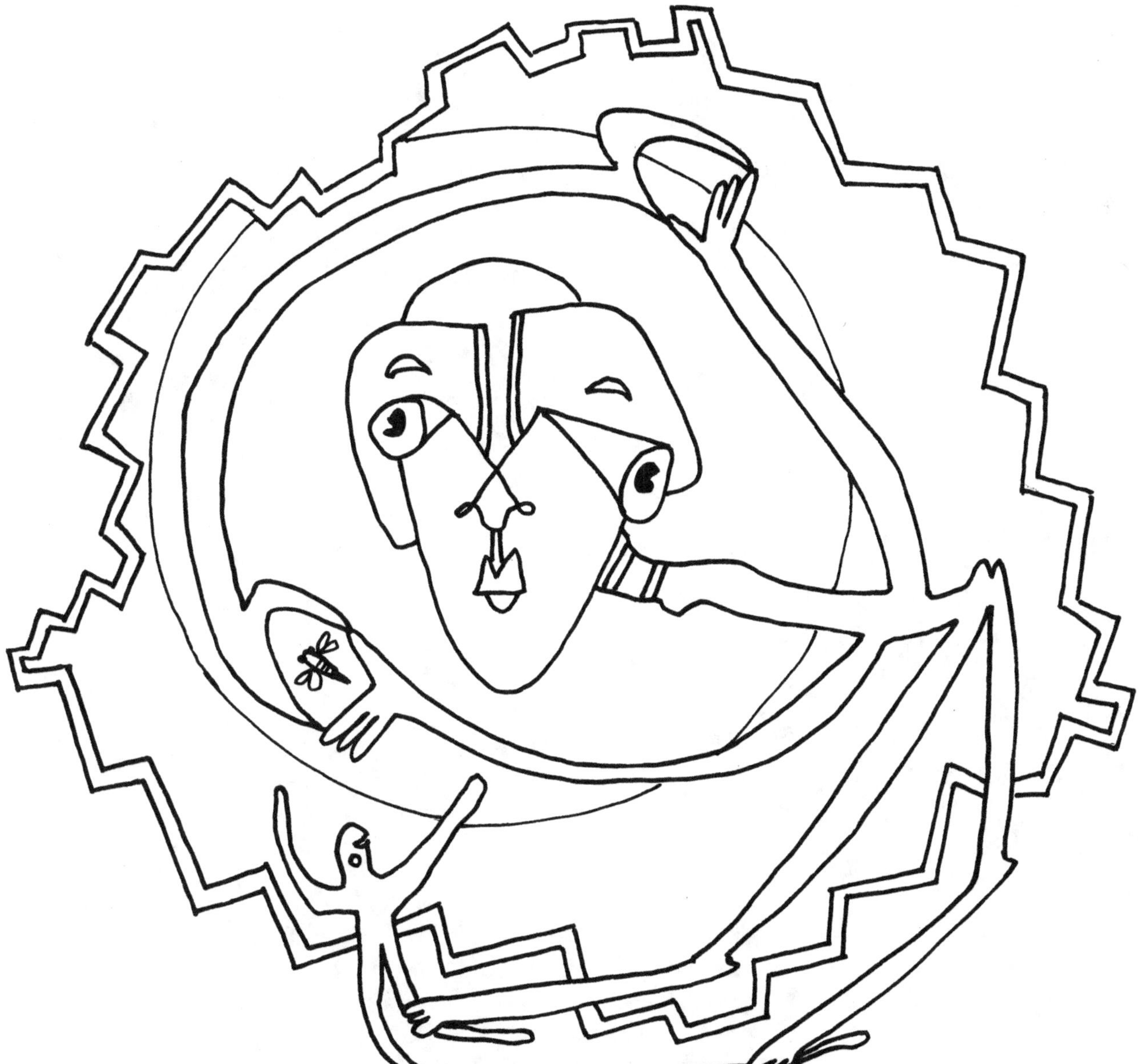

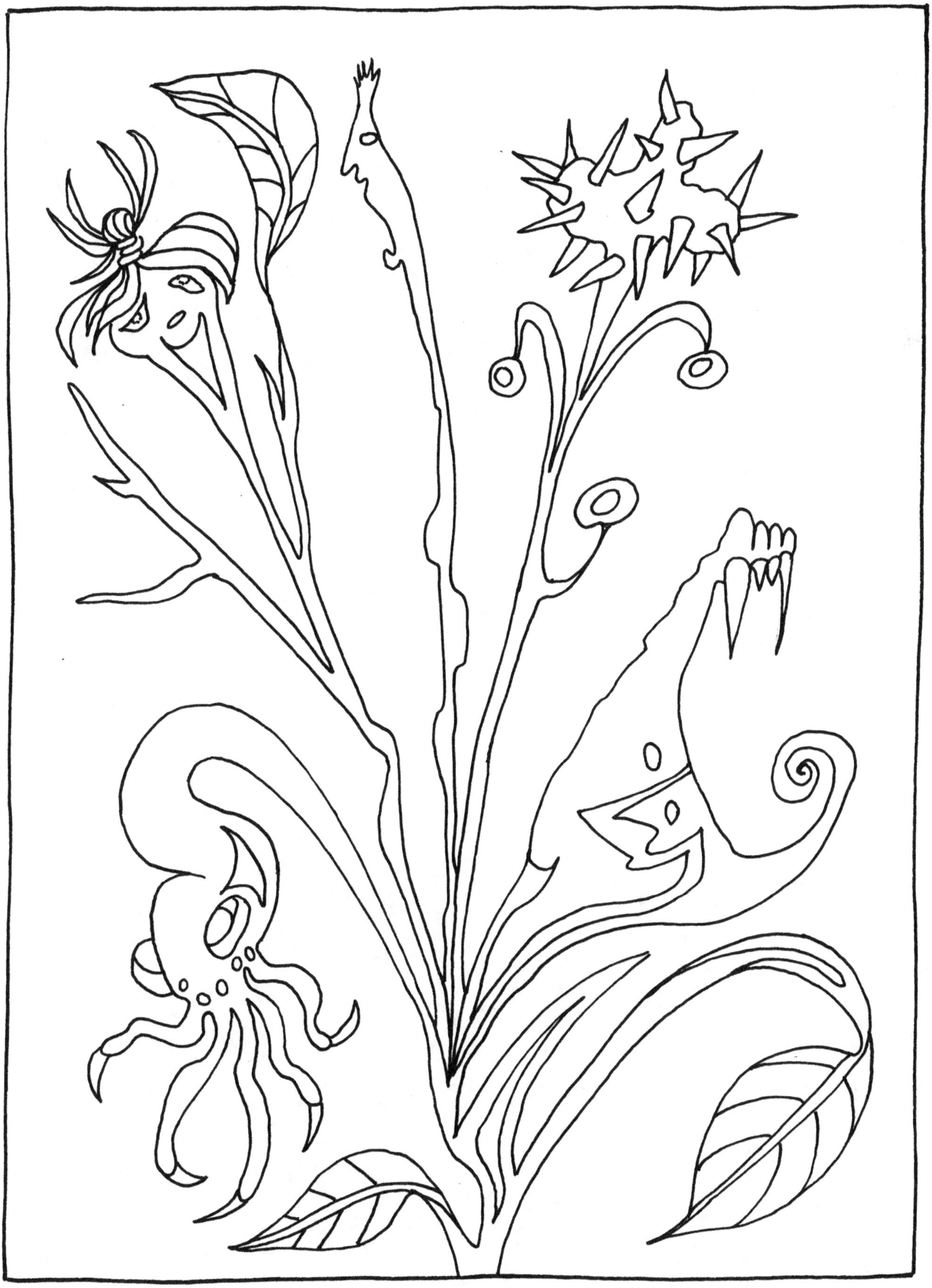

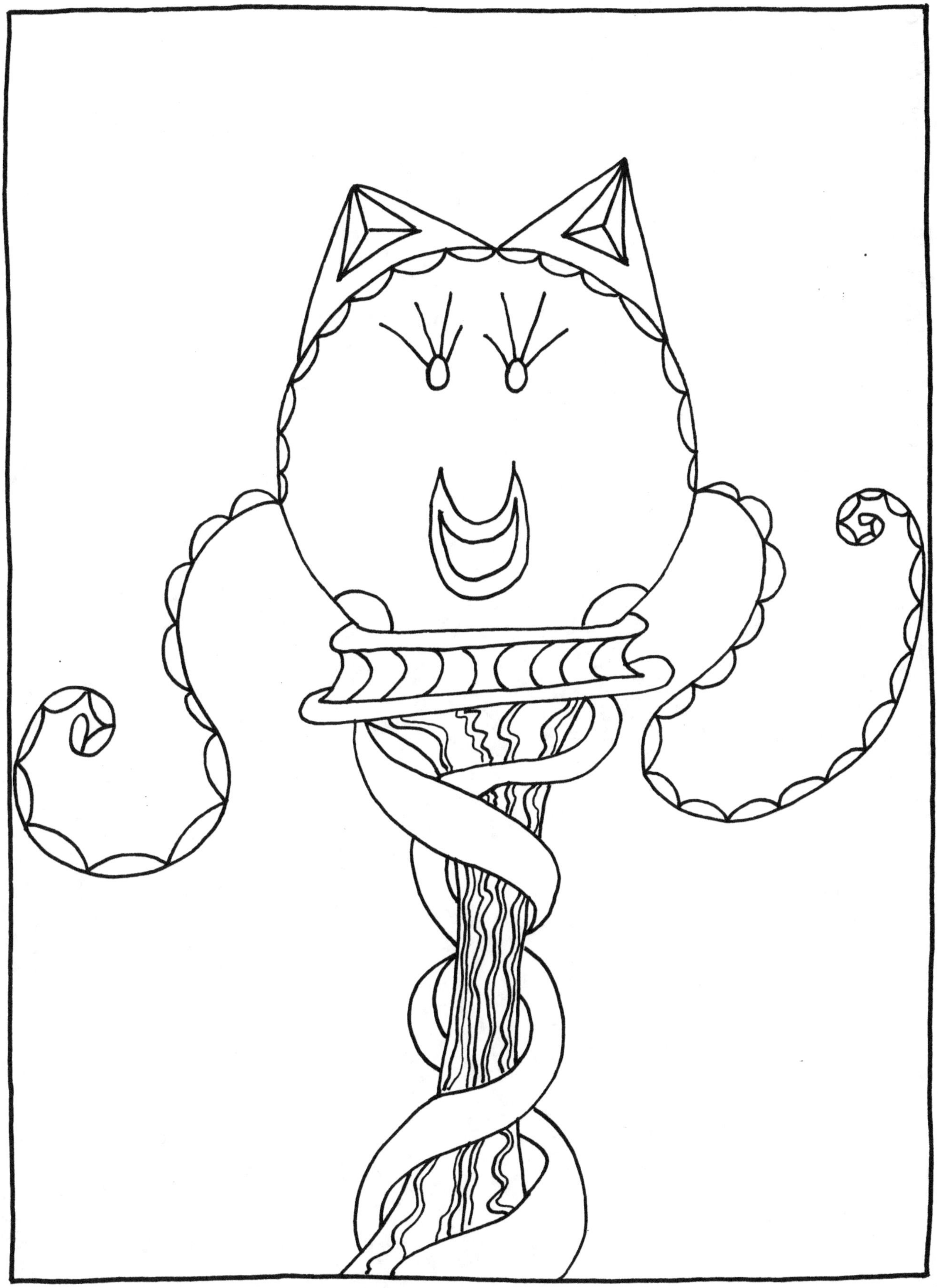

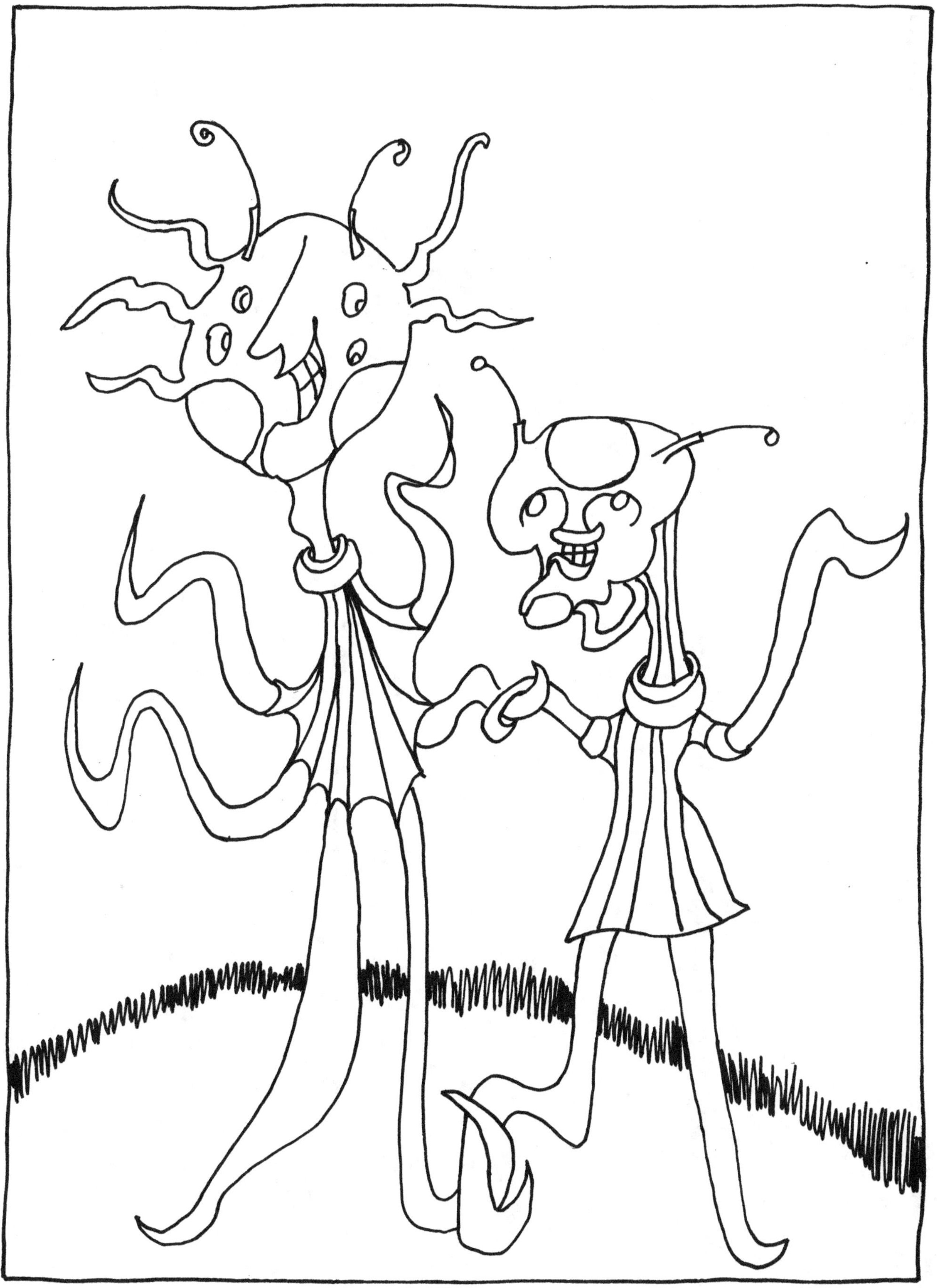

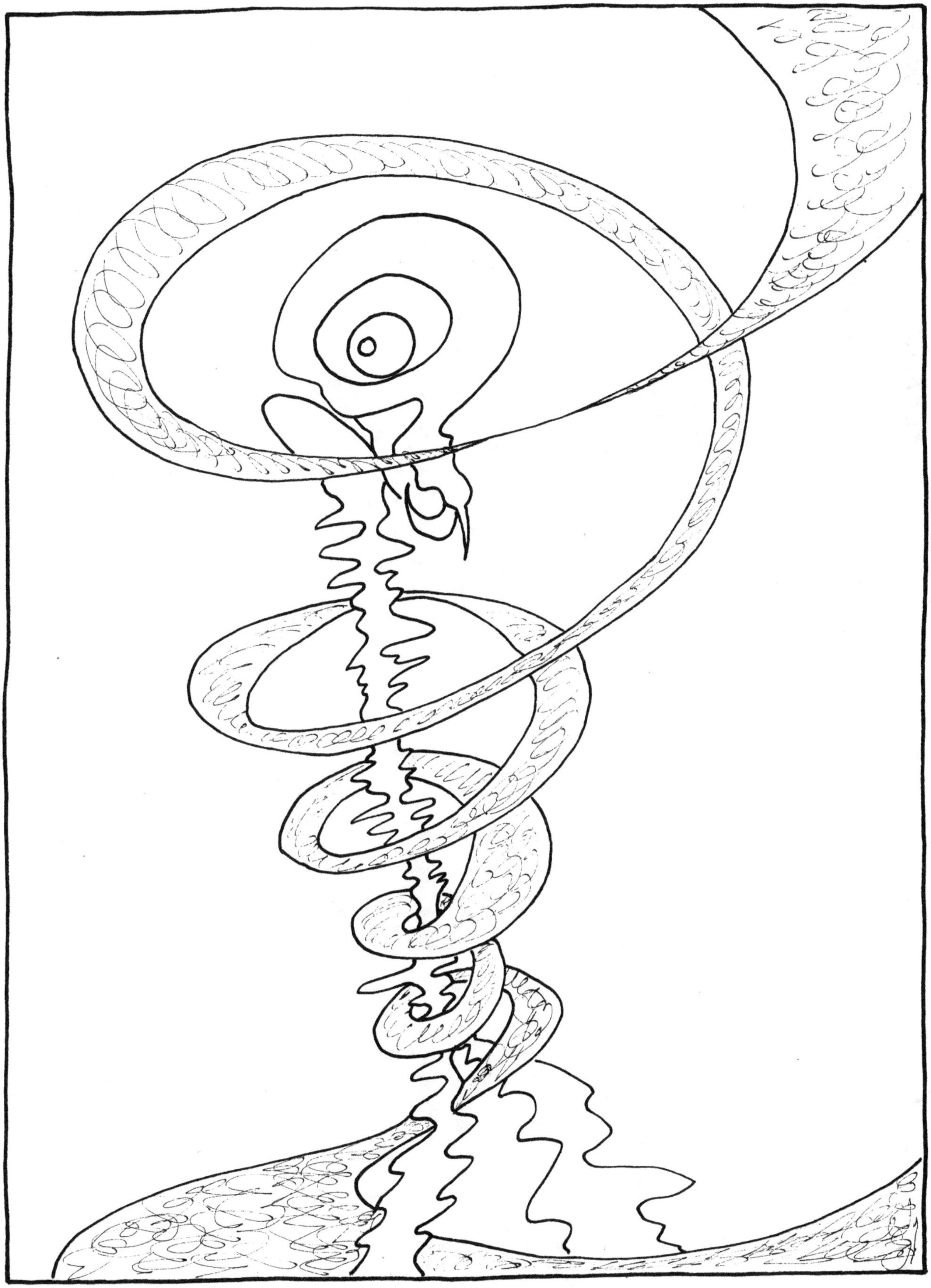

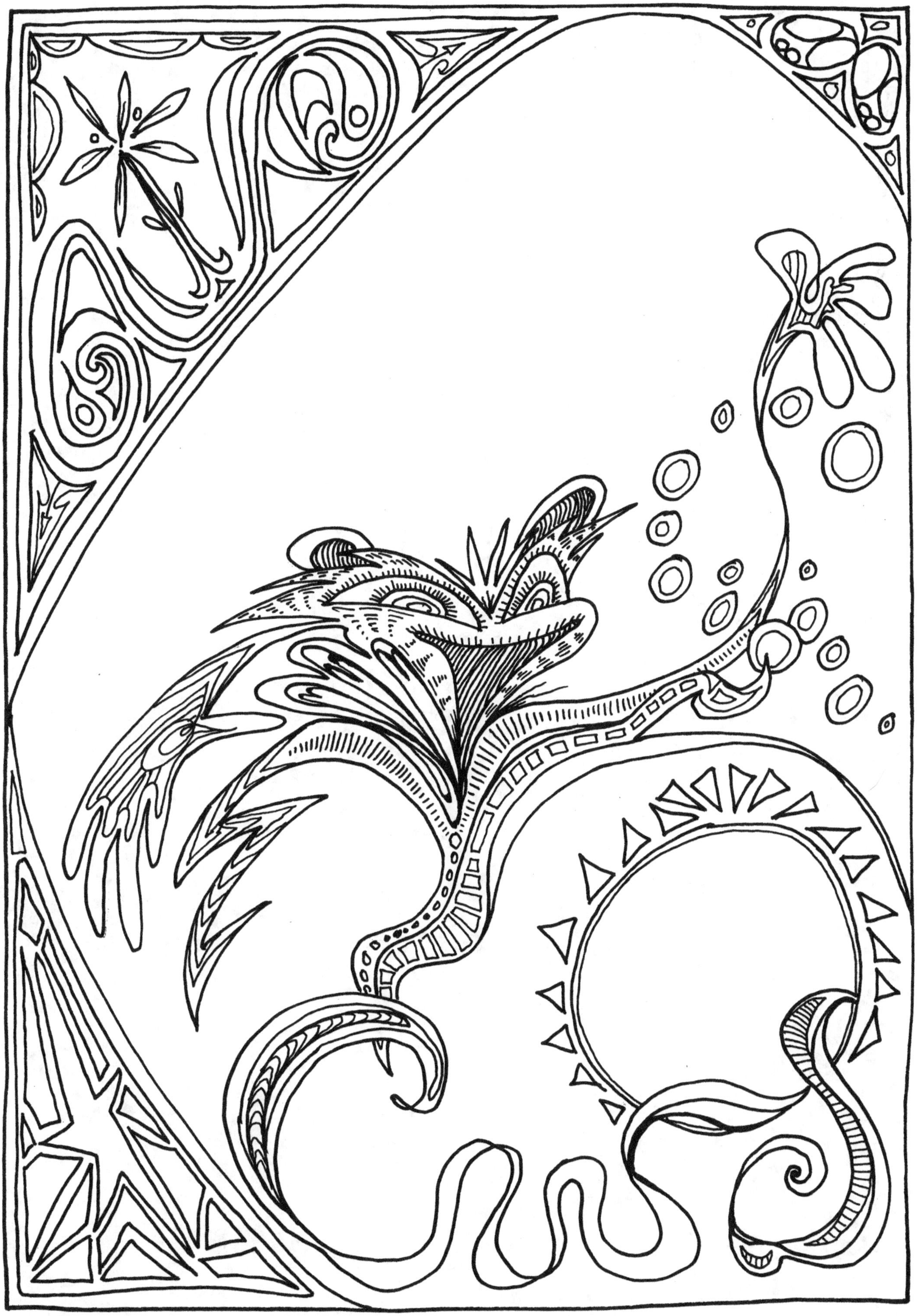

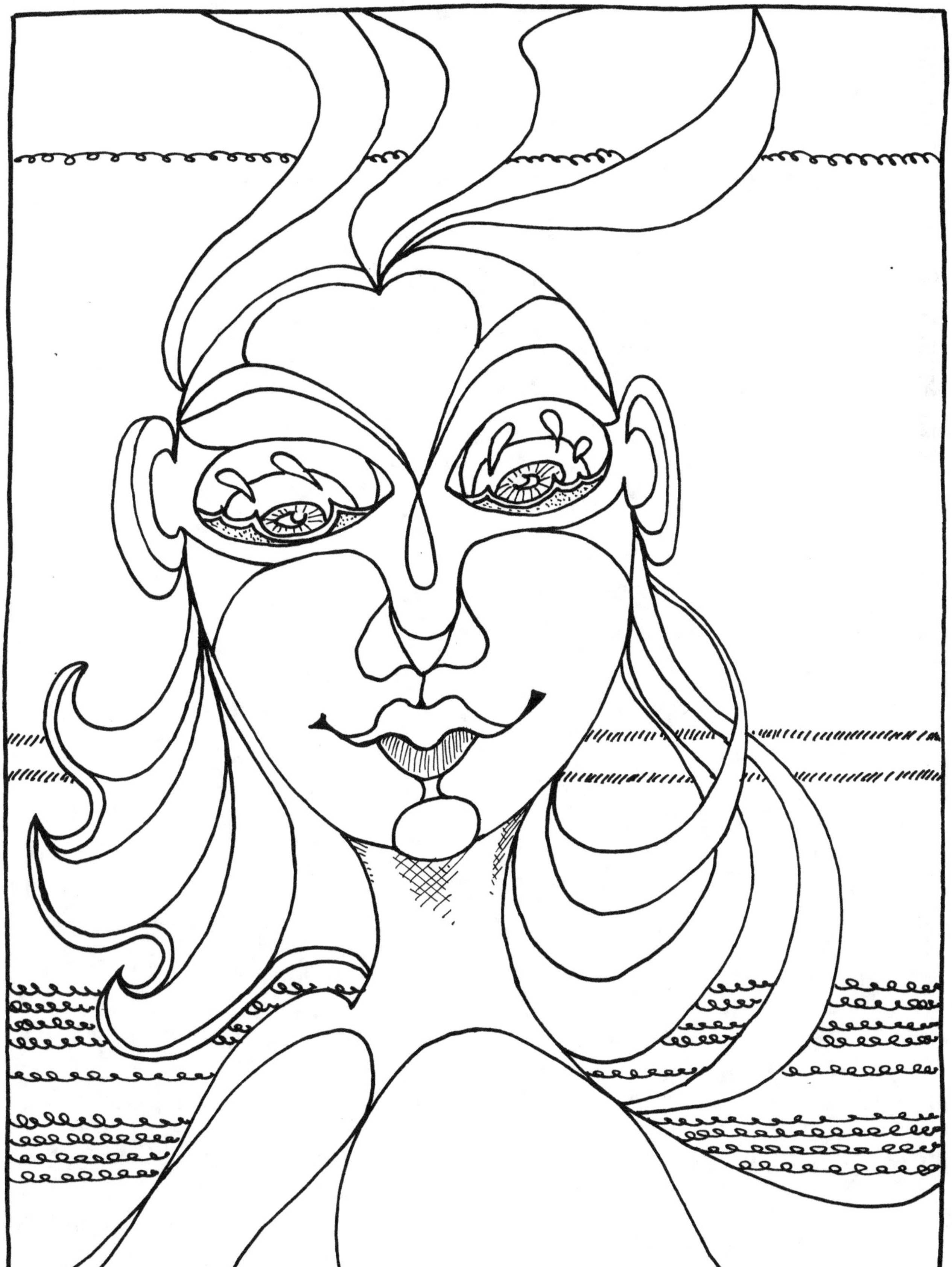

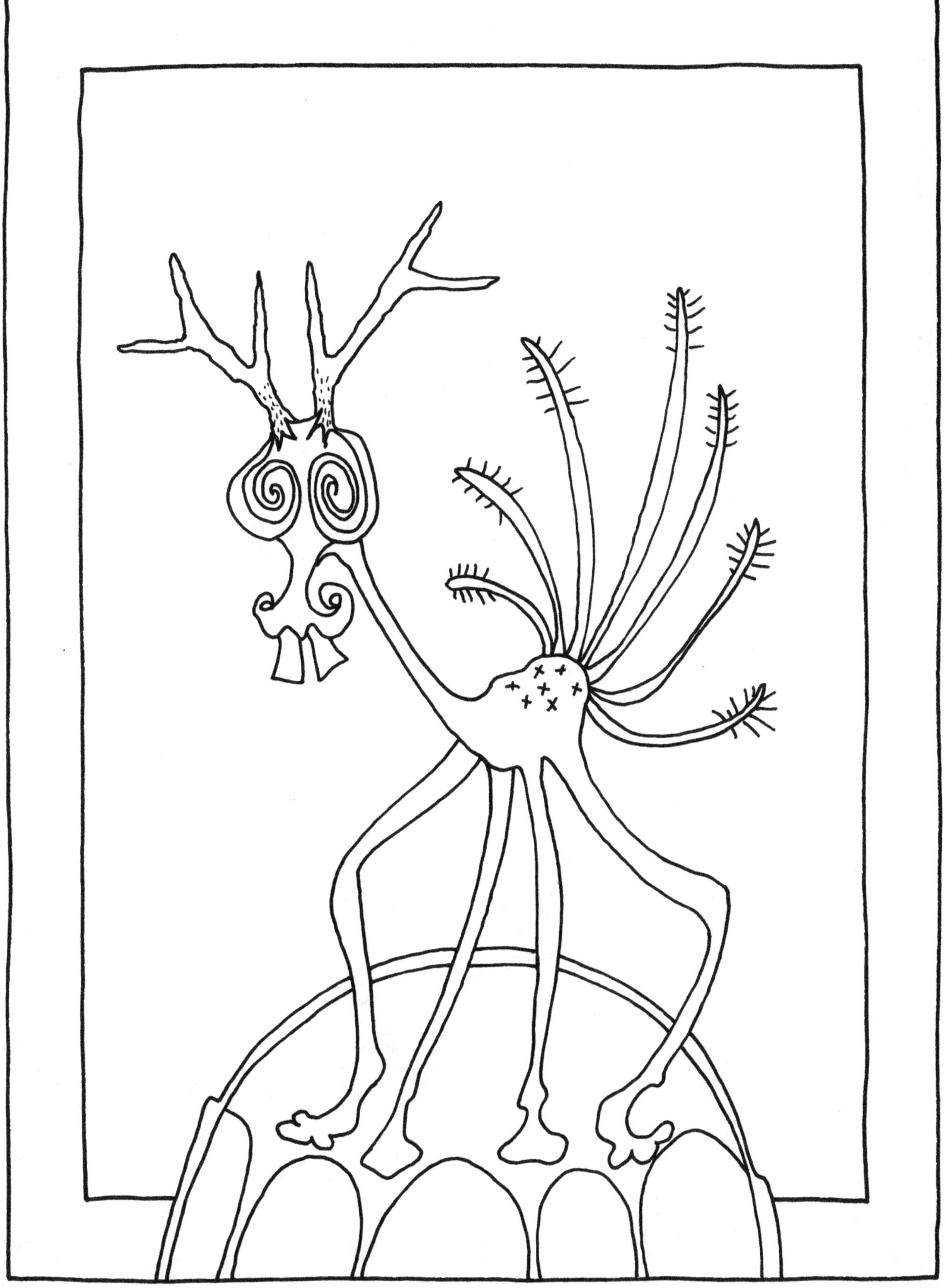

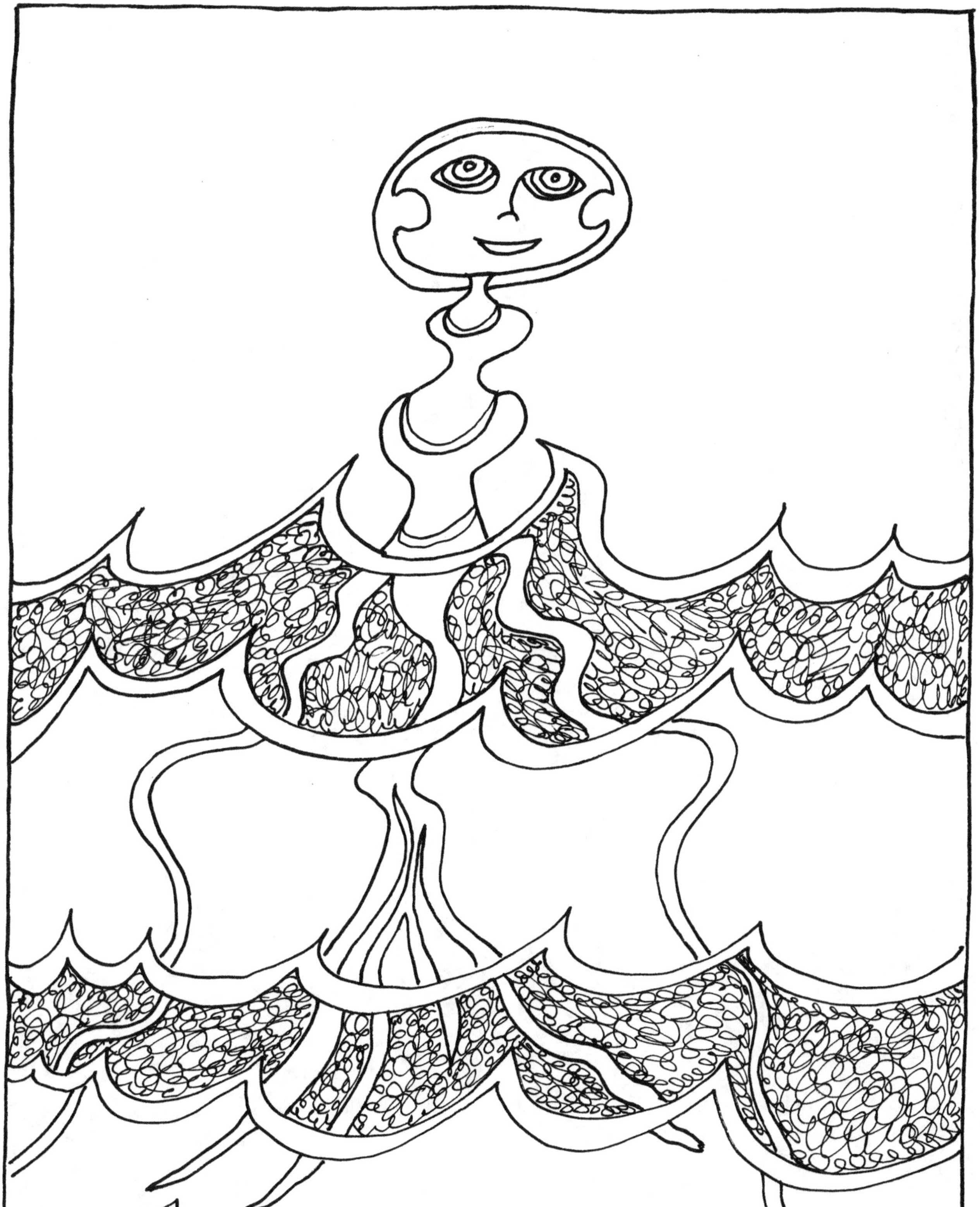

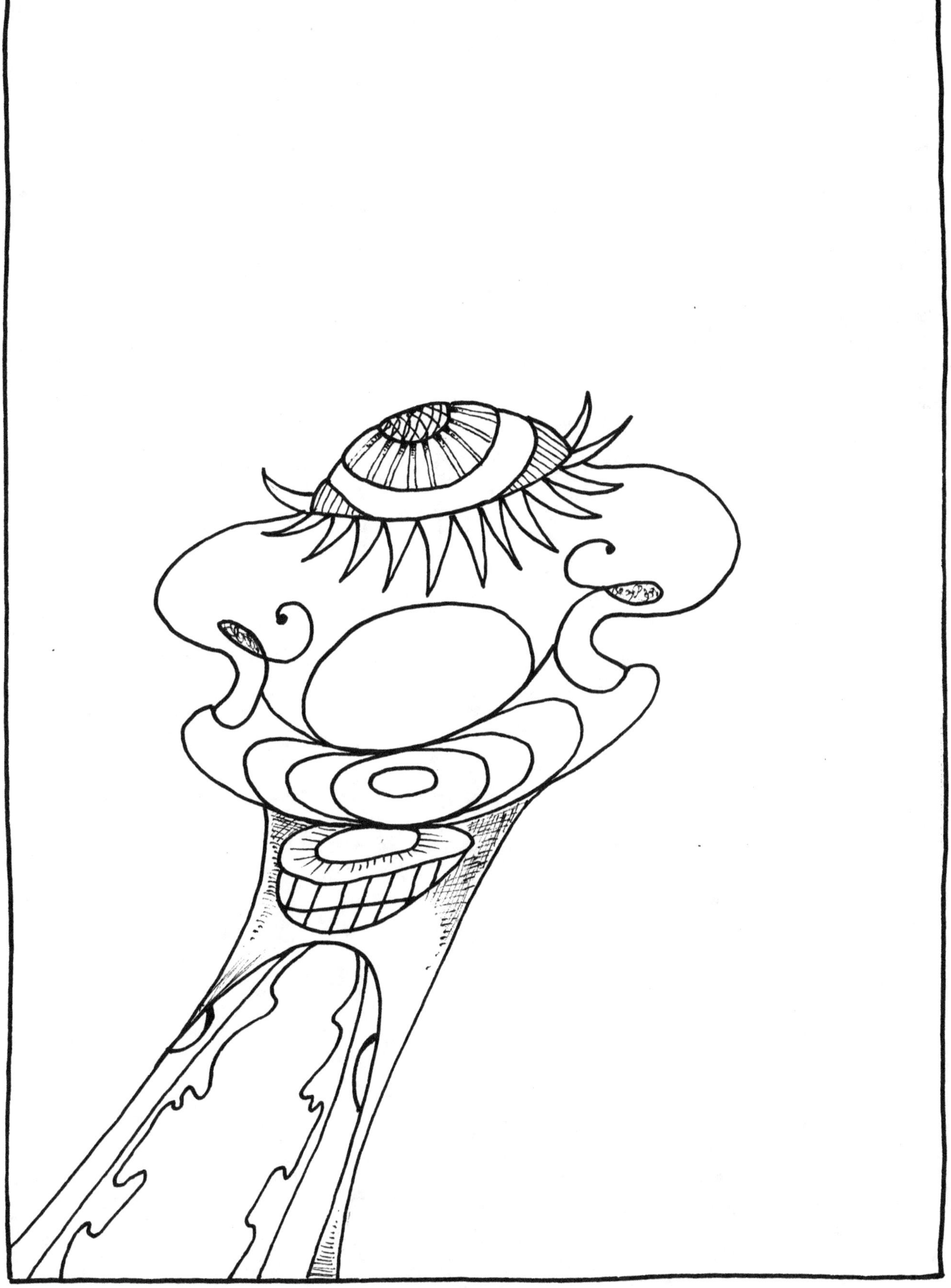

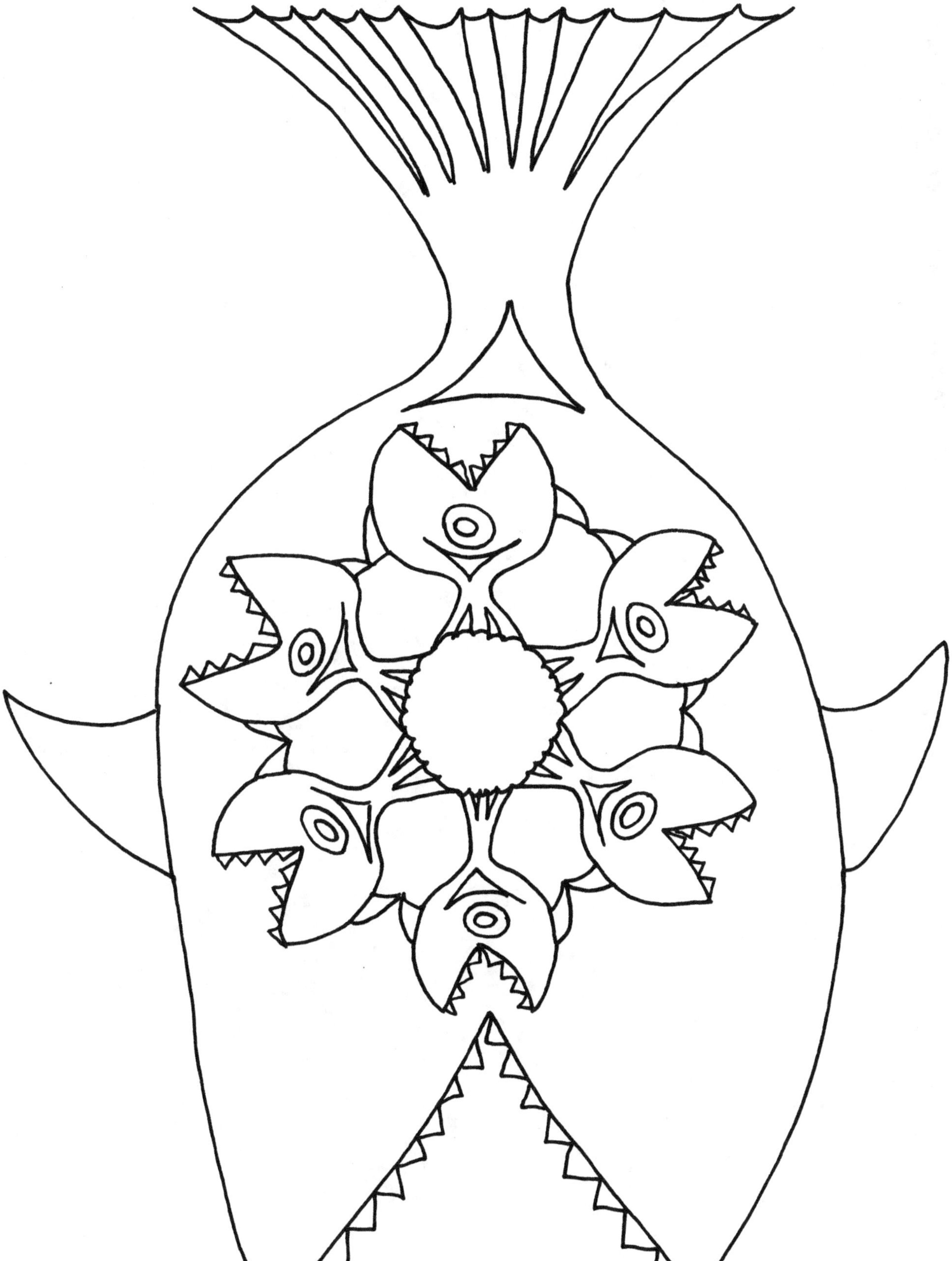

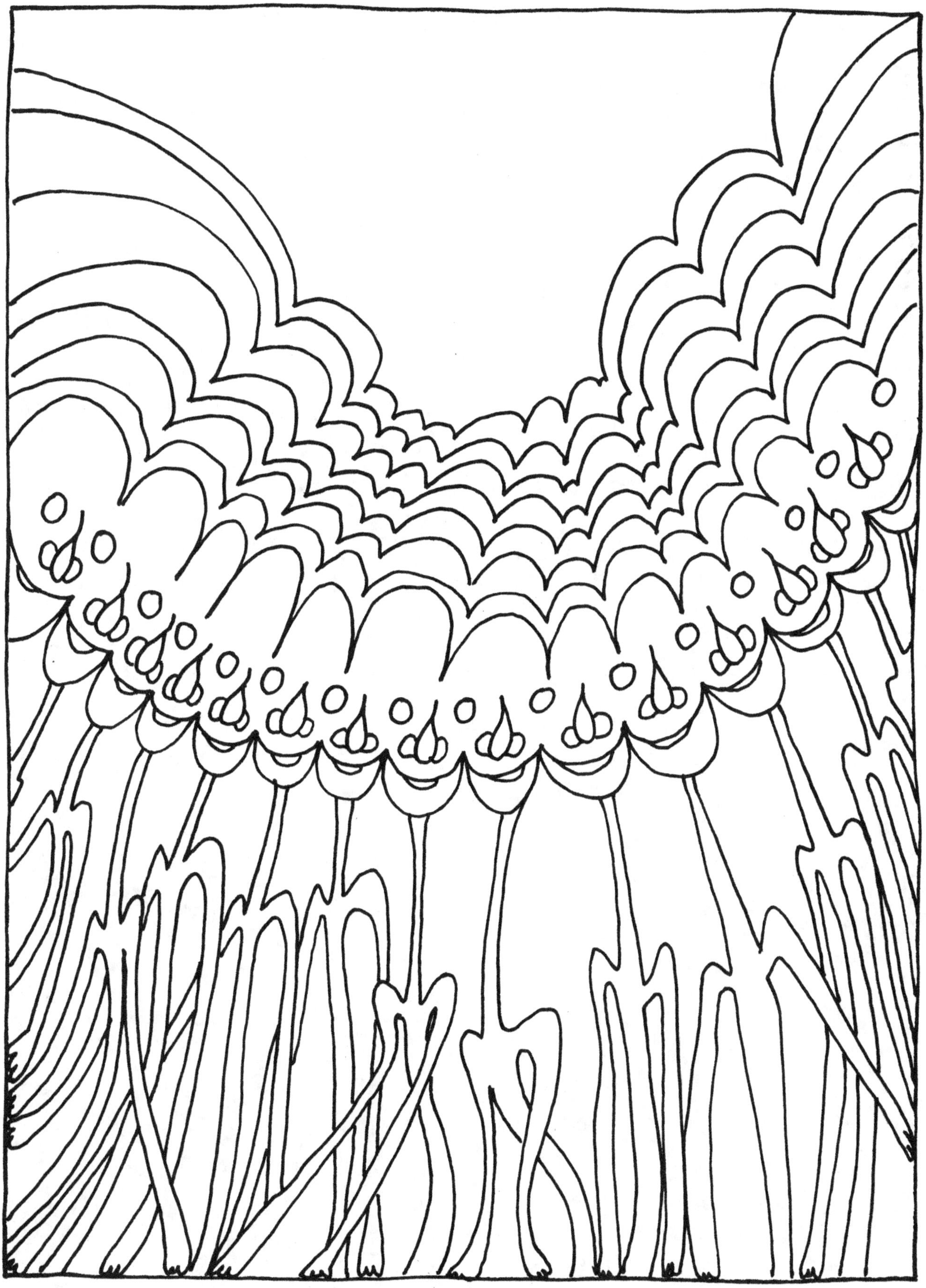

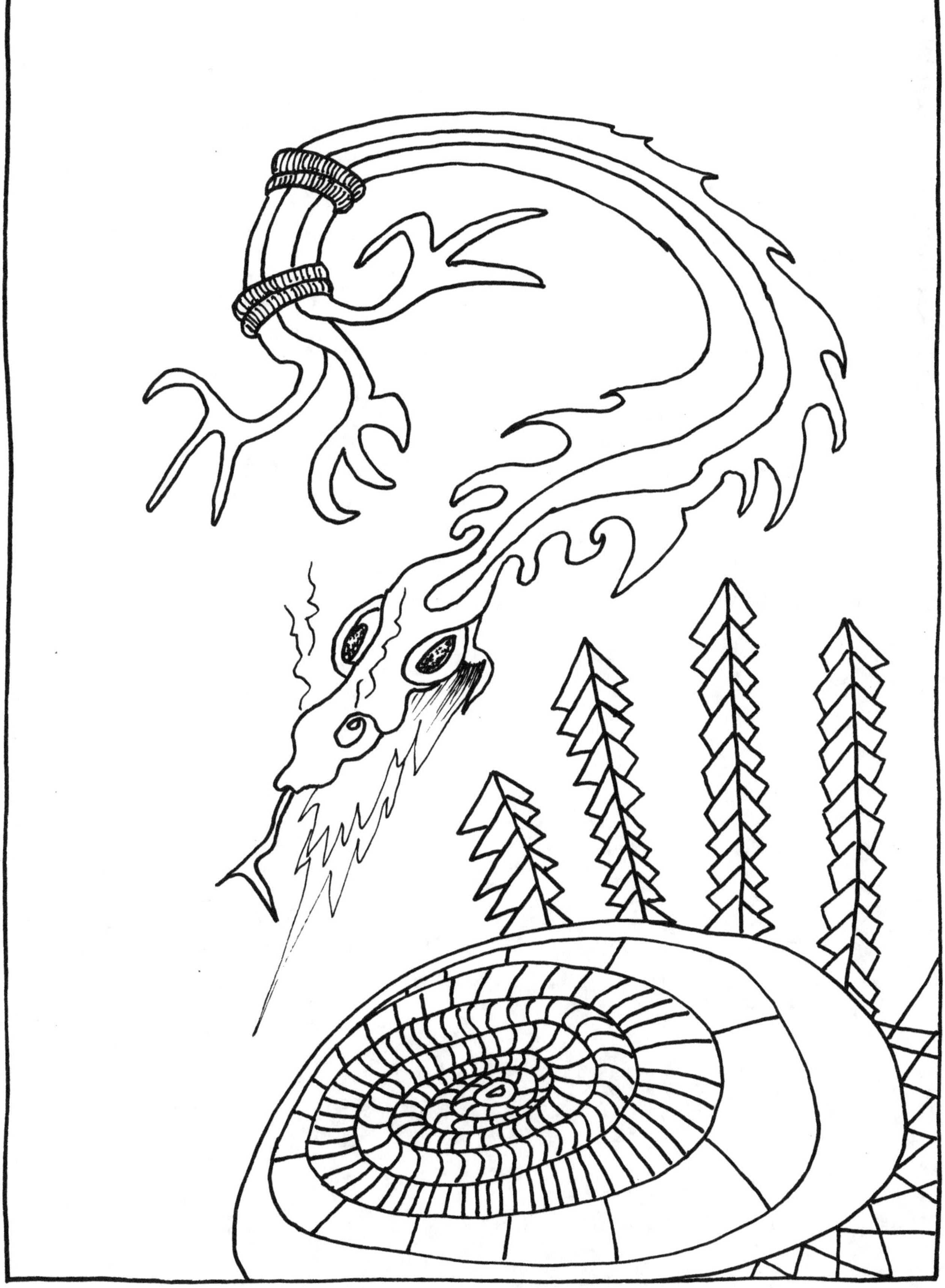

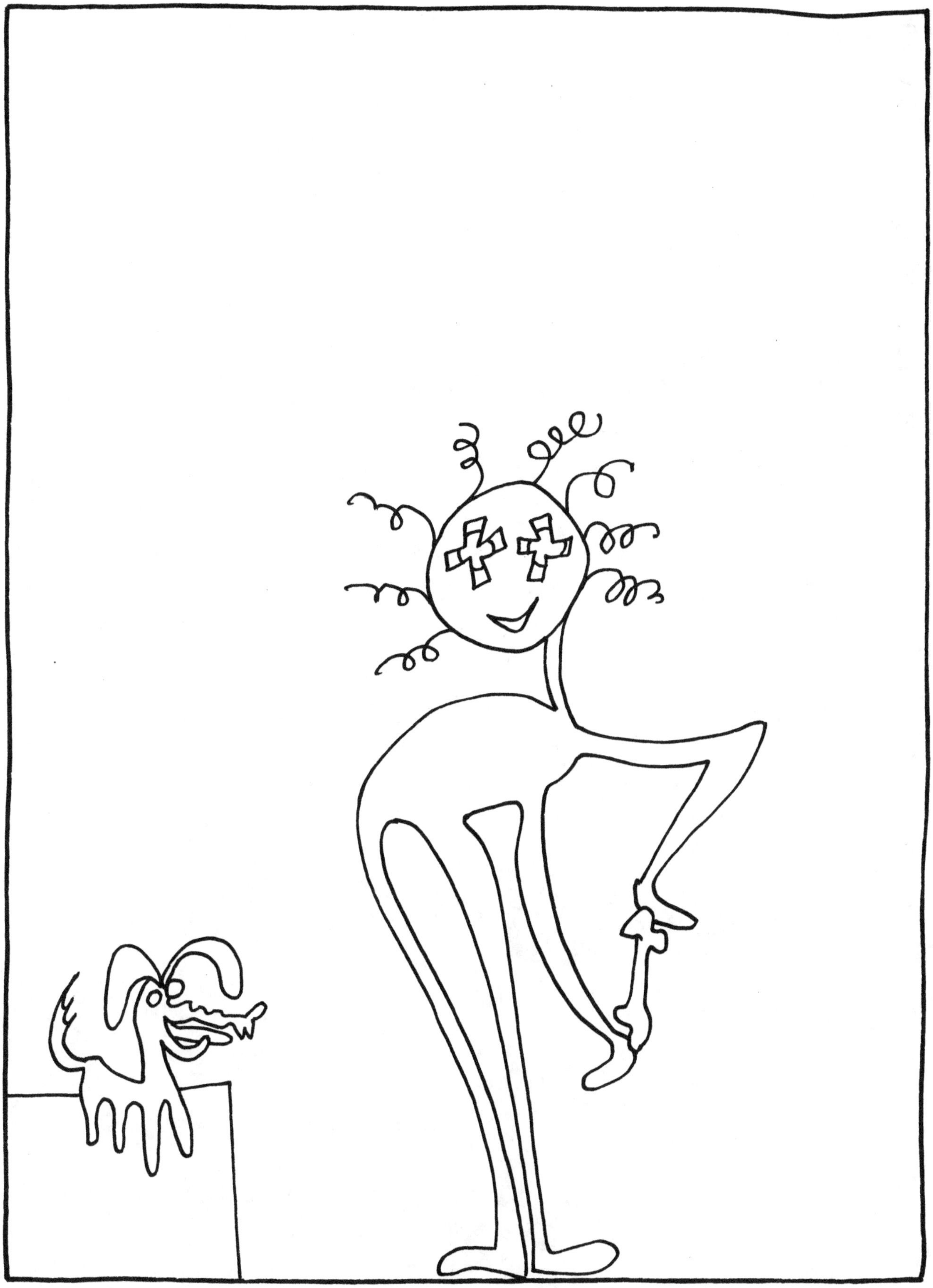

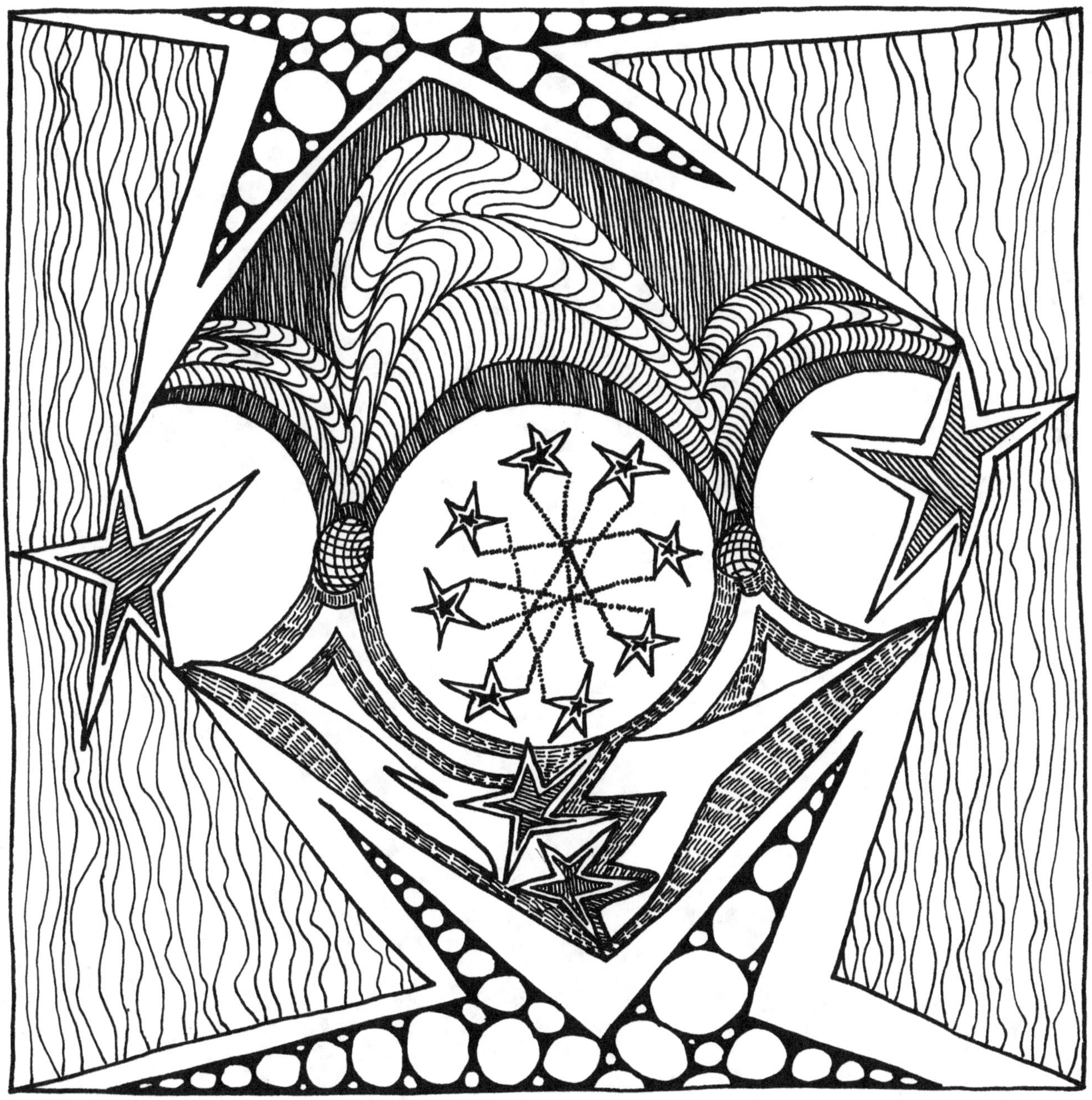

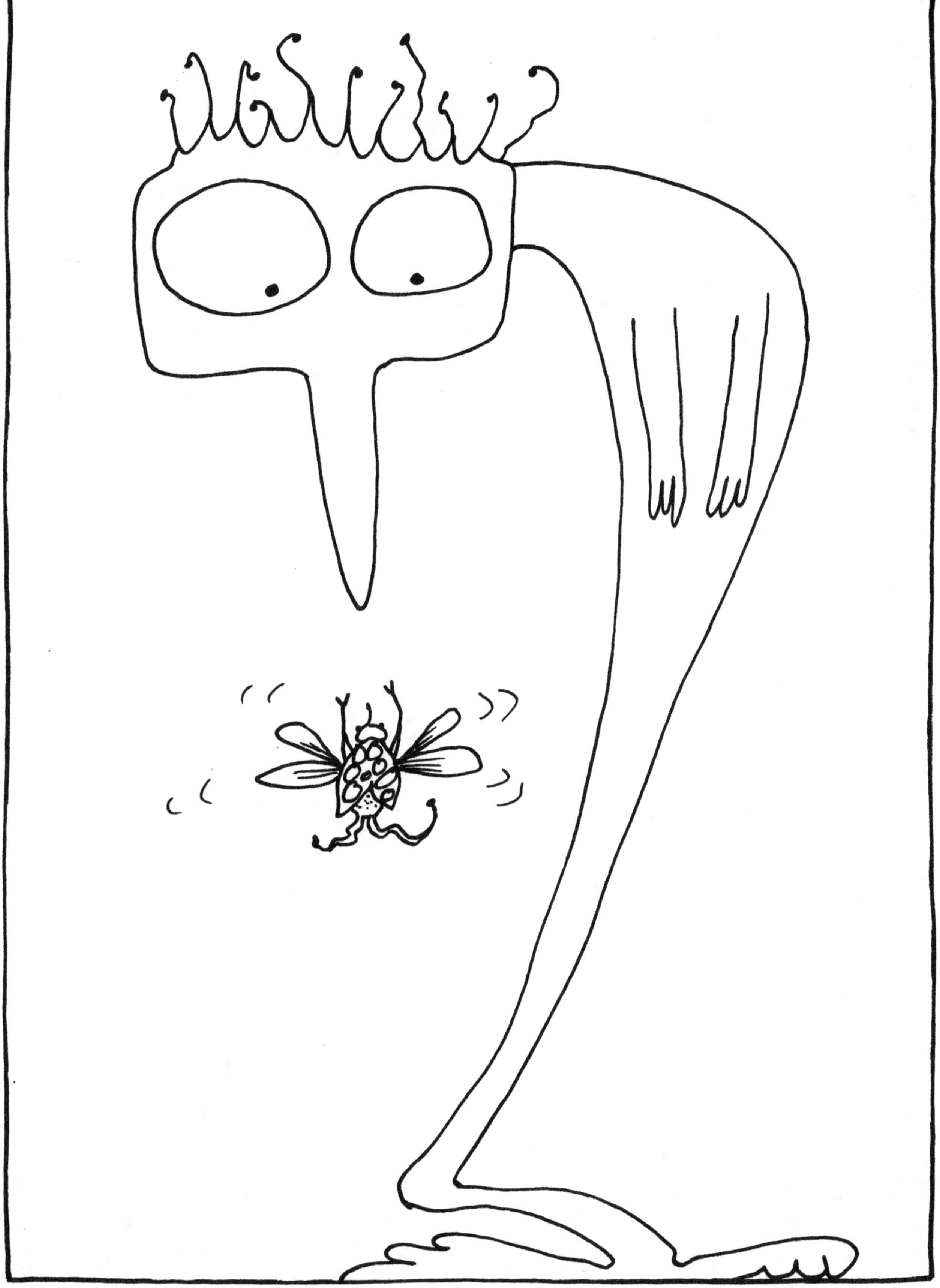

CREATURA #6 ©2019 Joan Worth

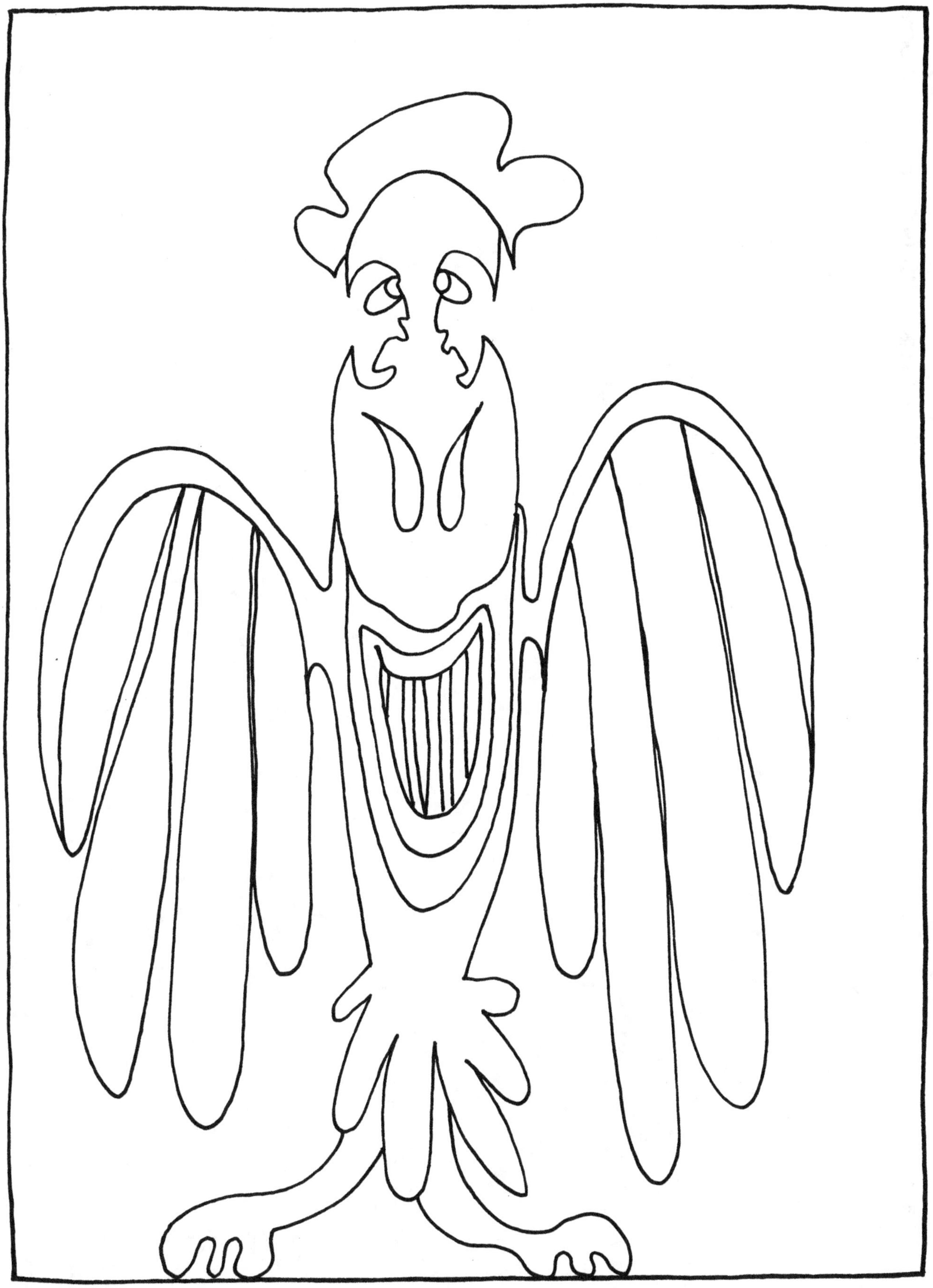

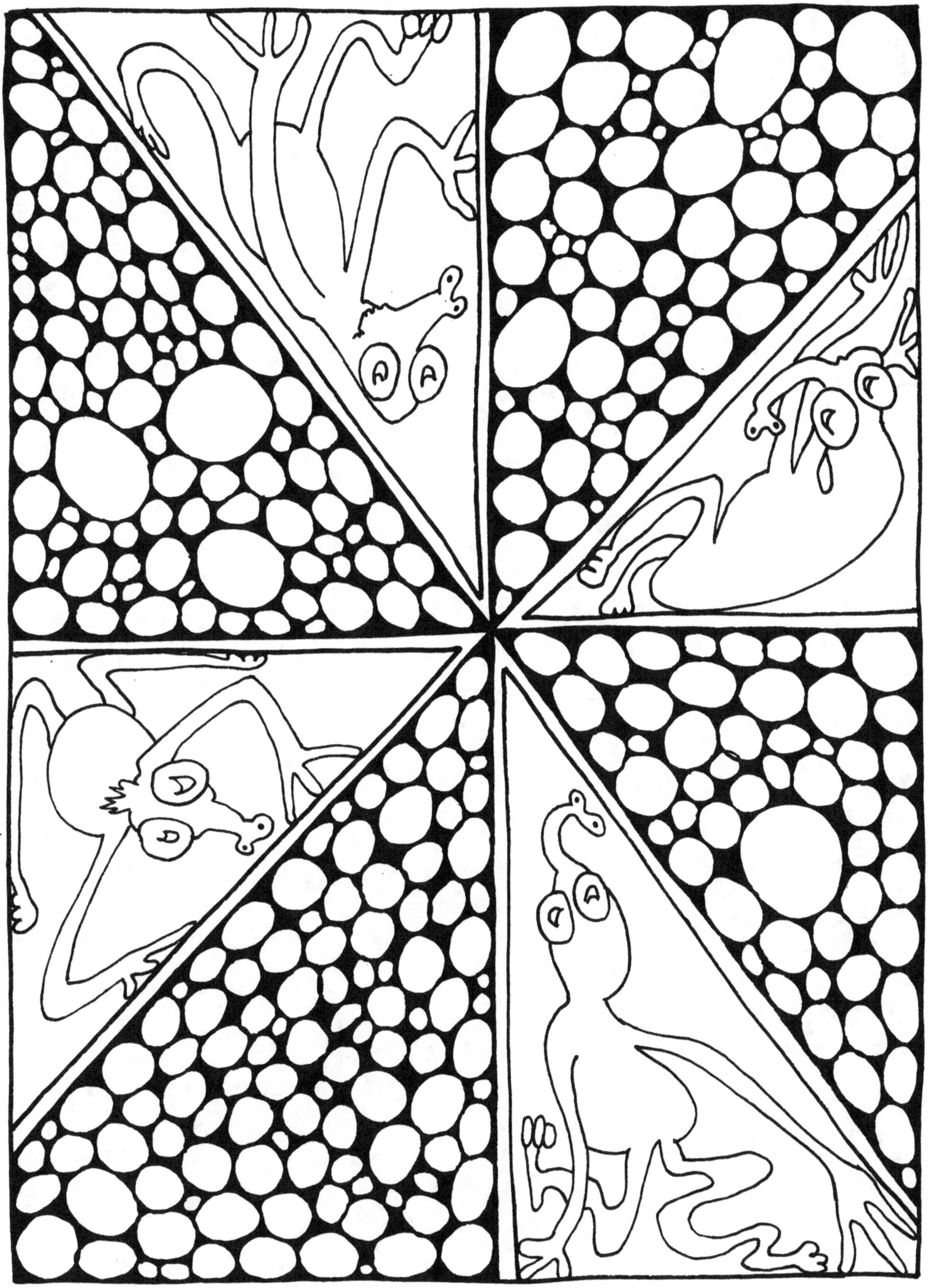

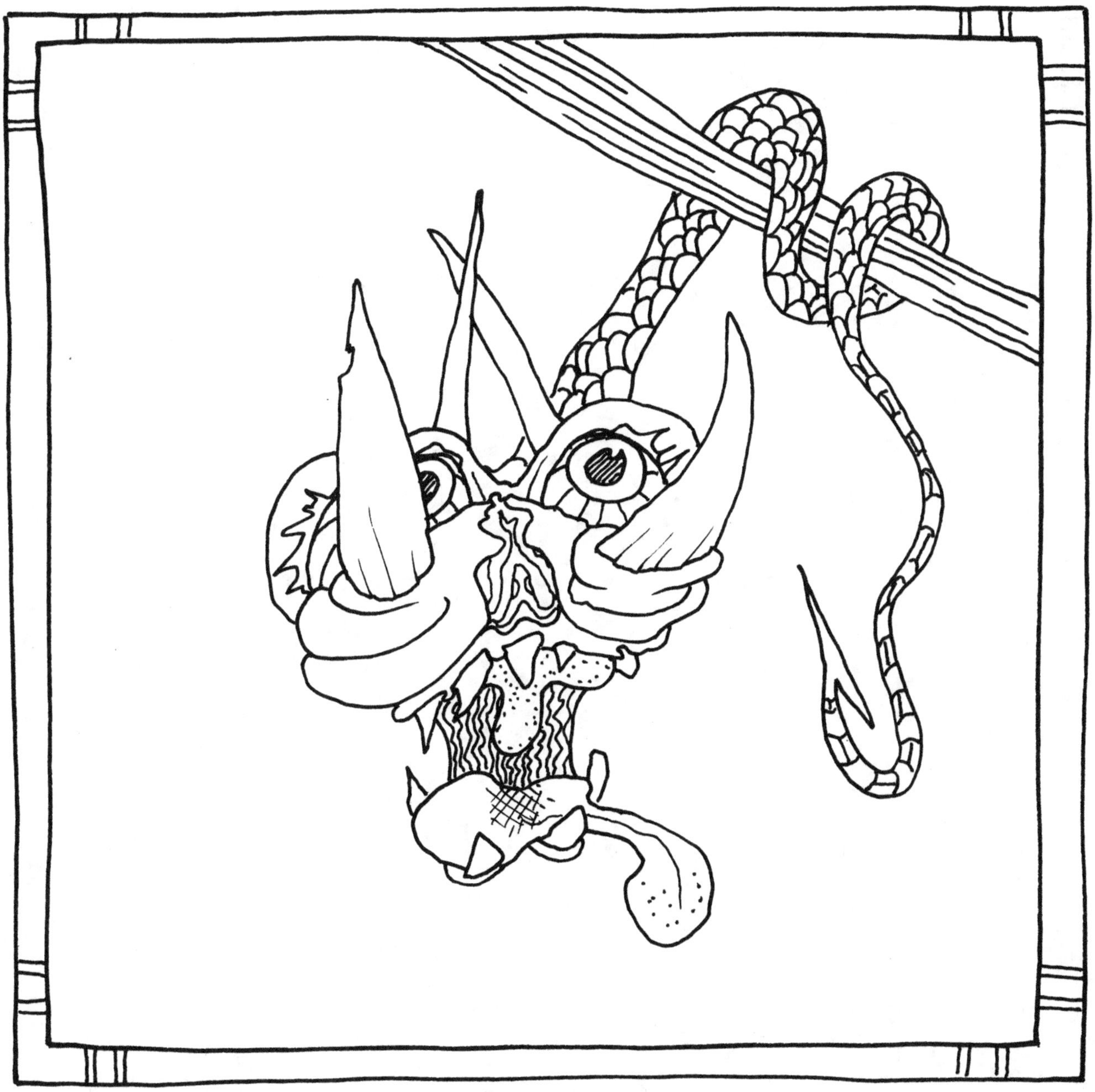

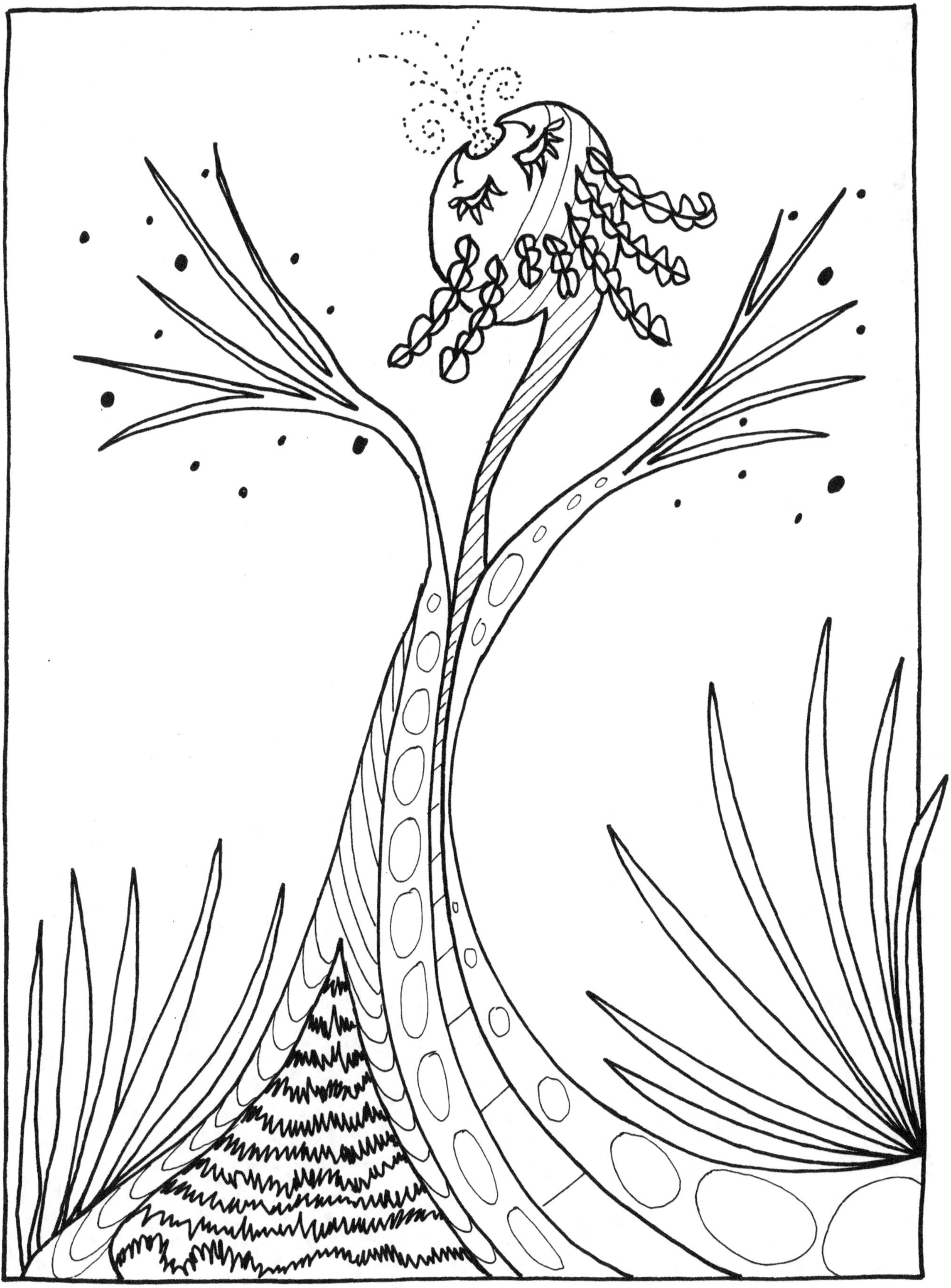

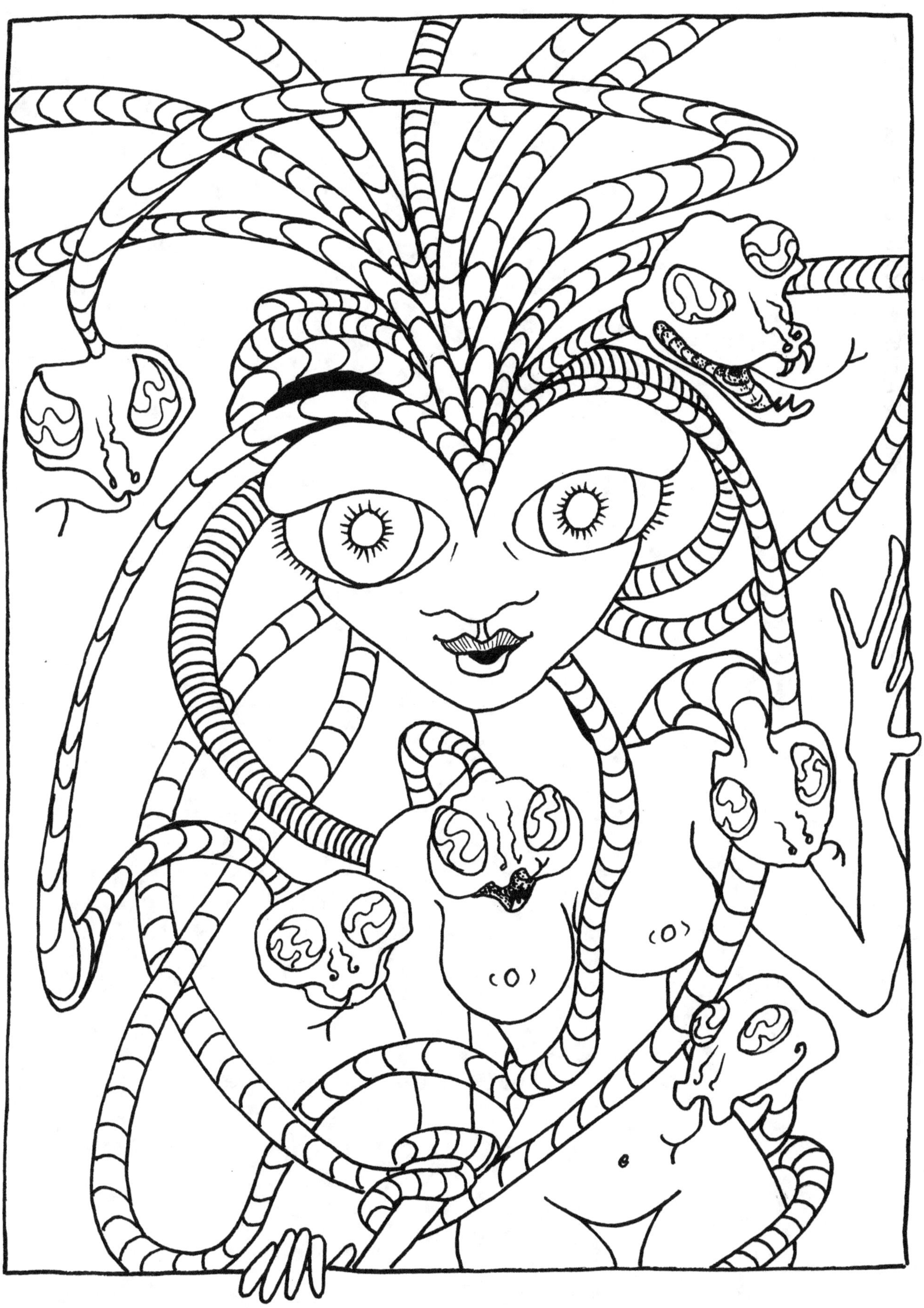

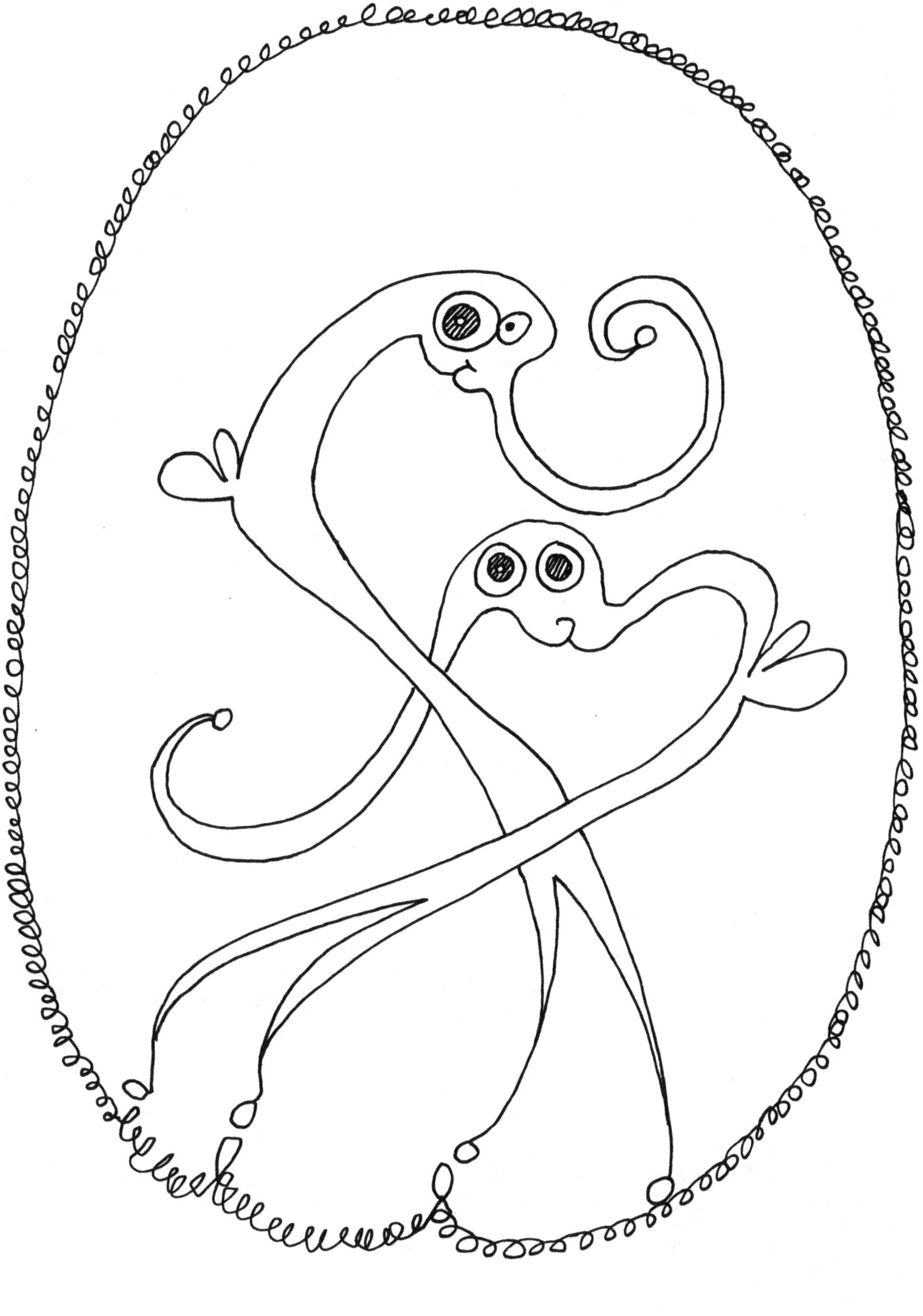

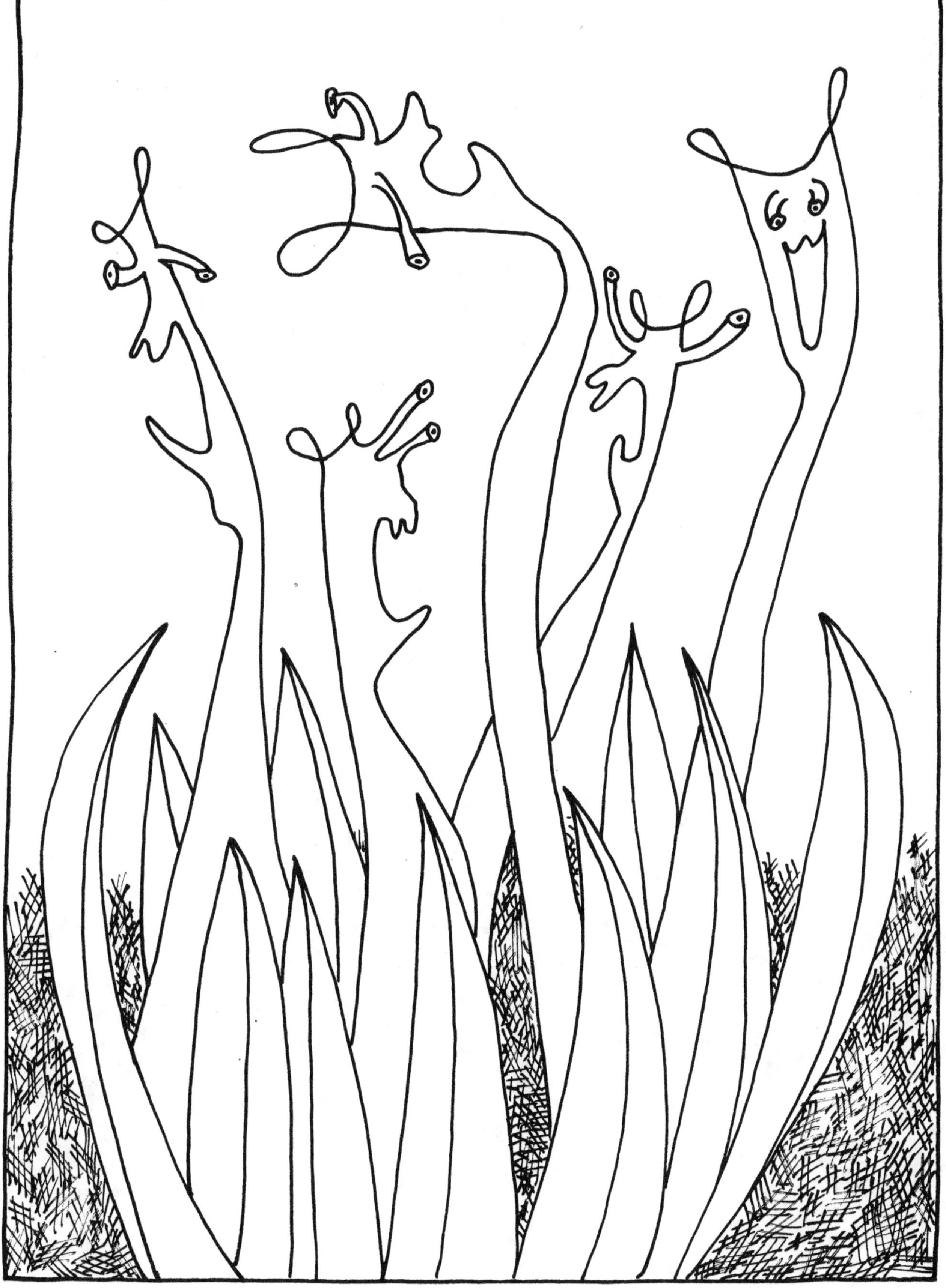

CREATURA #6 ©2019 Joan Worth

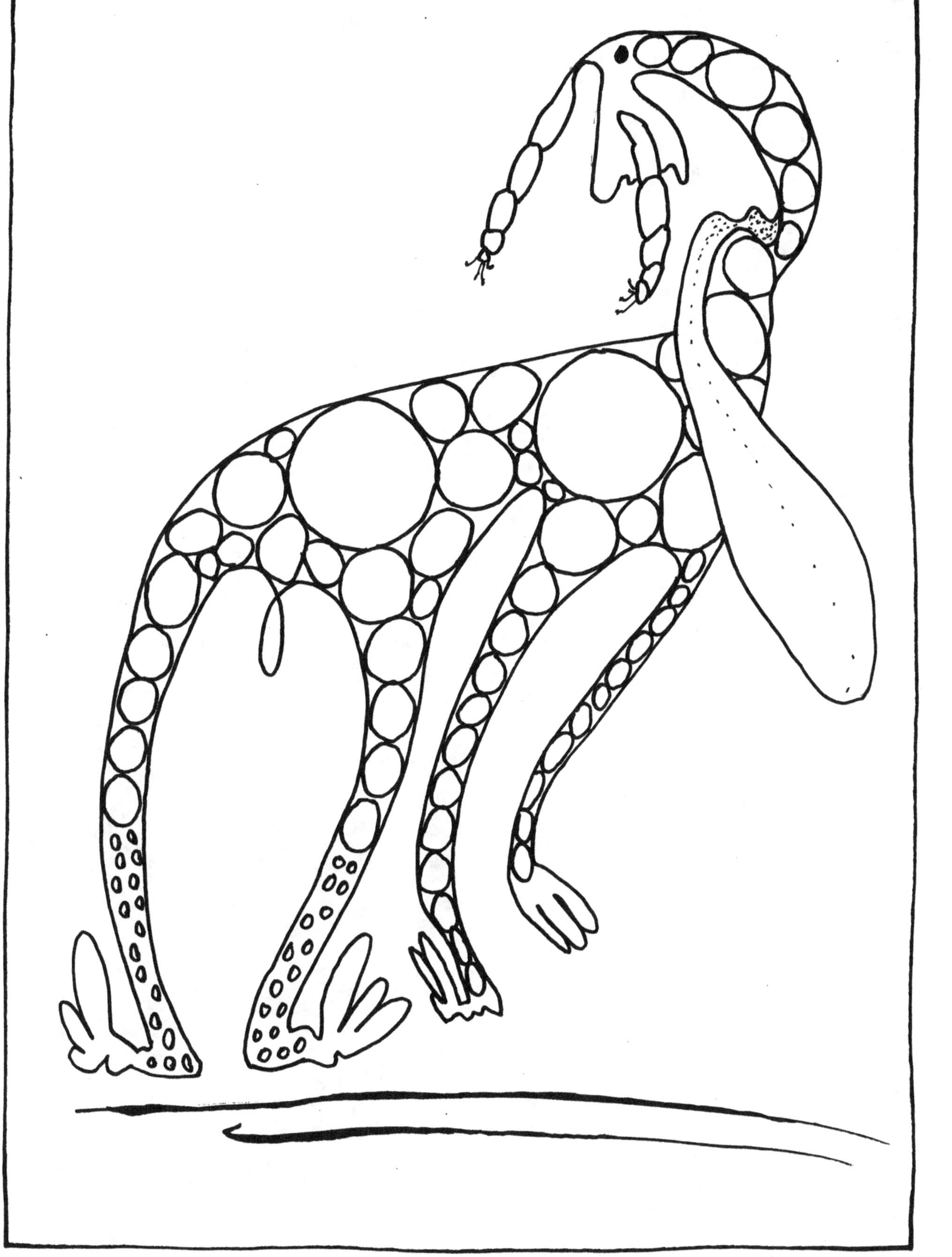

CREATURA #6

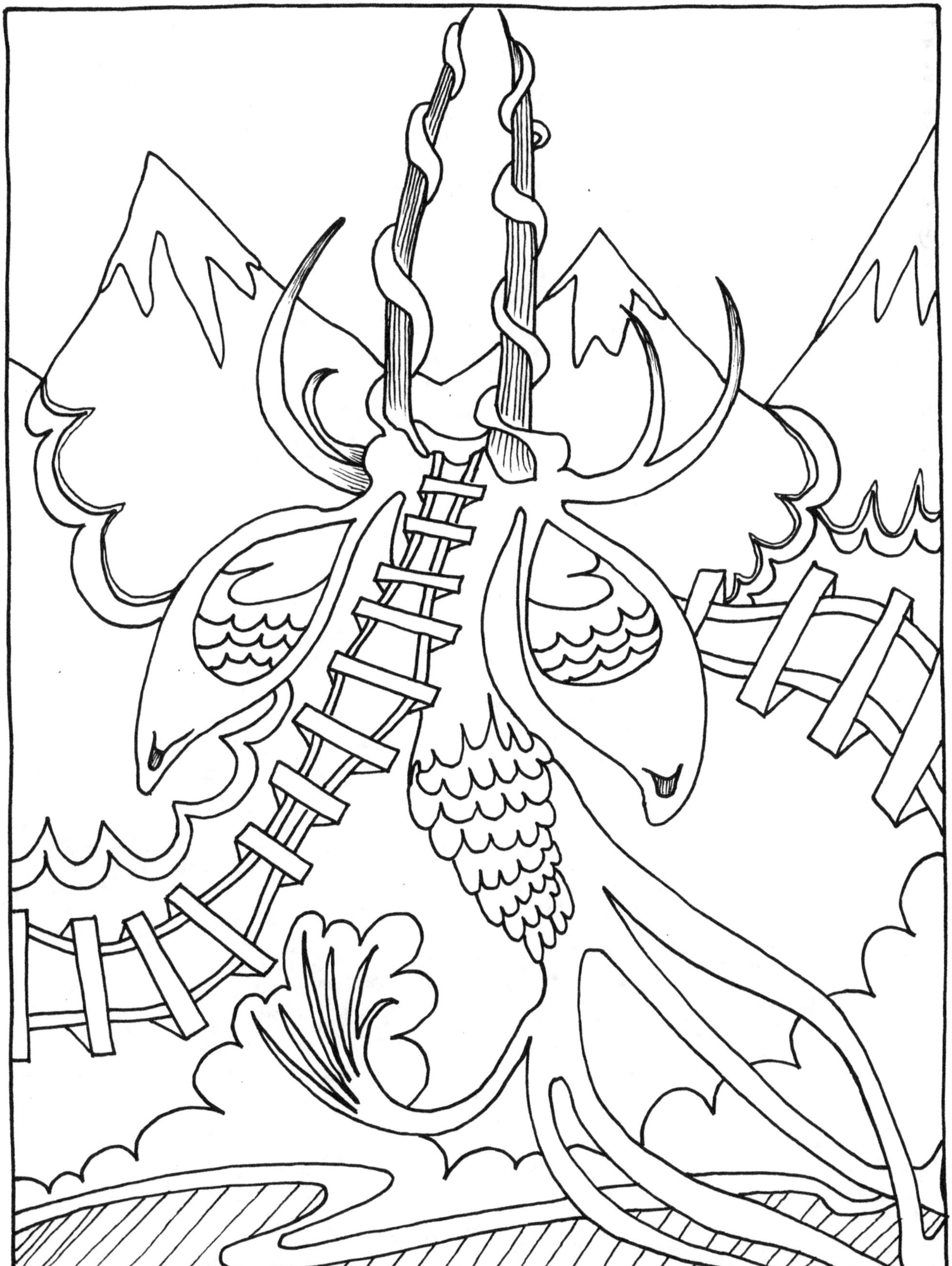

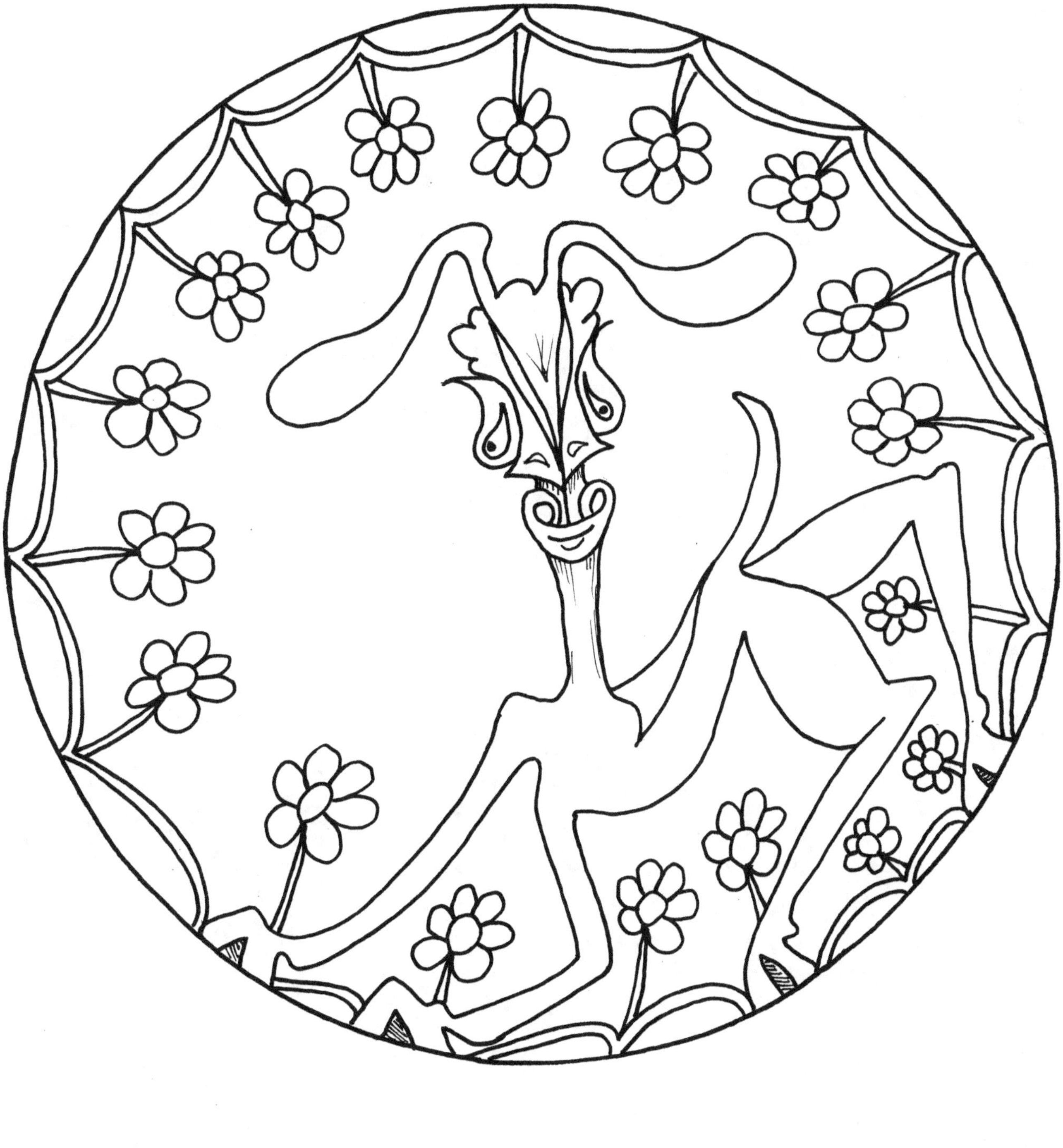

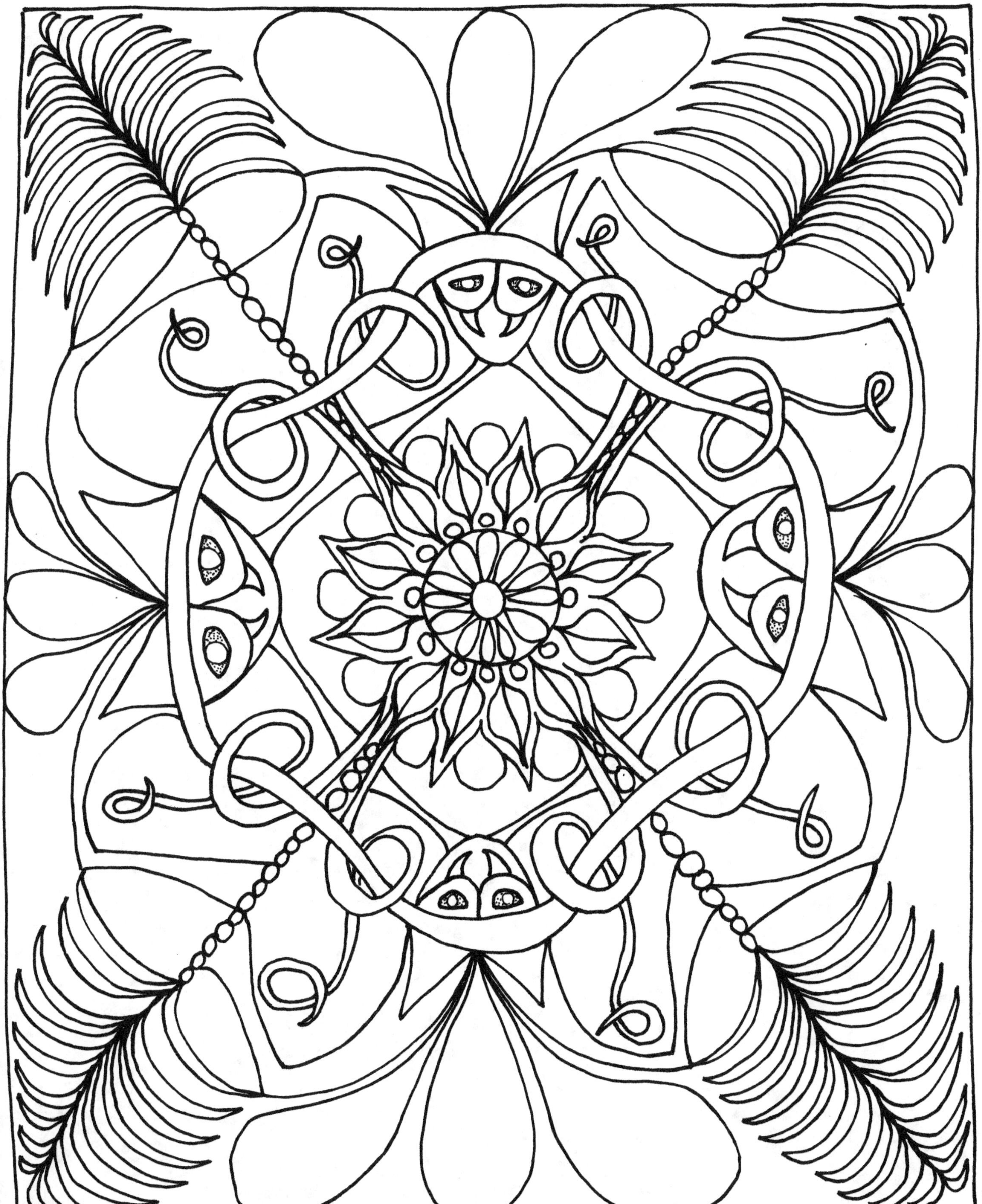

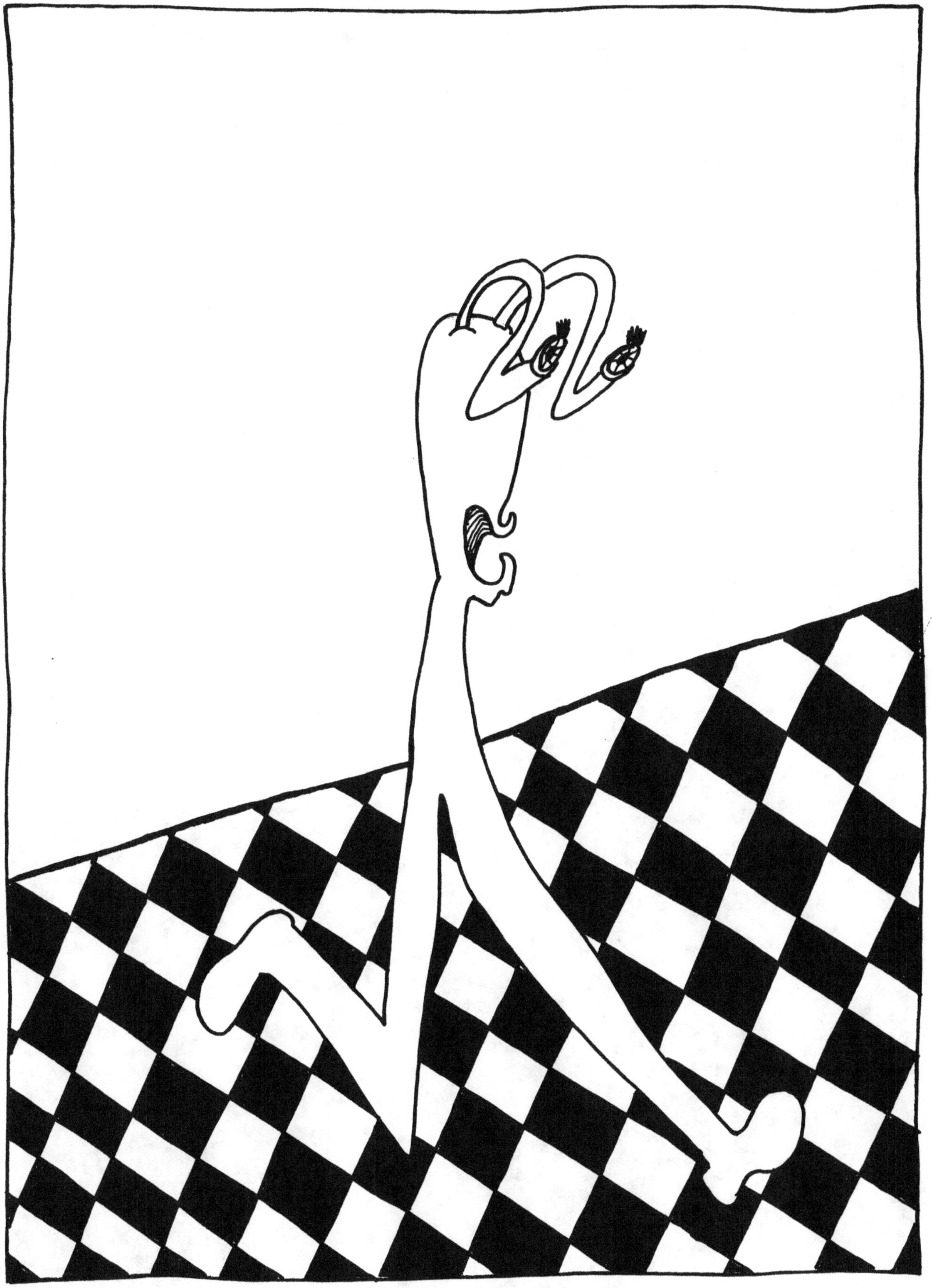

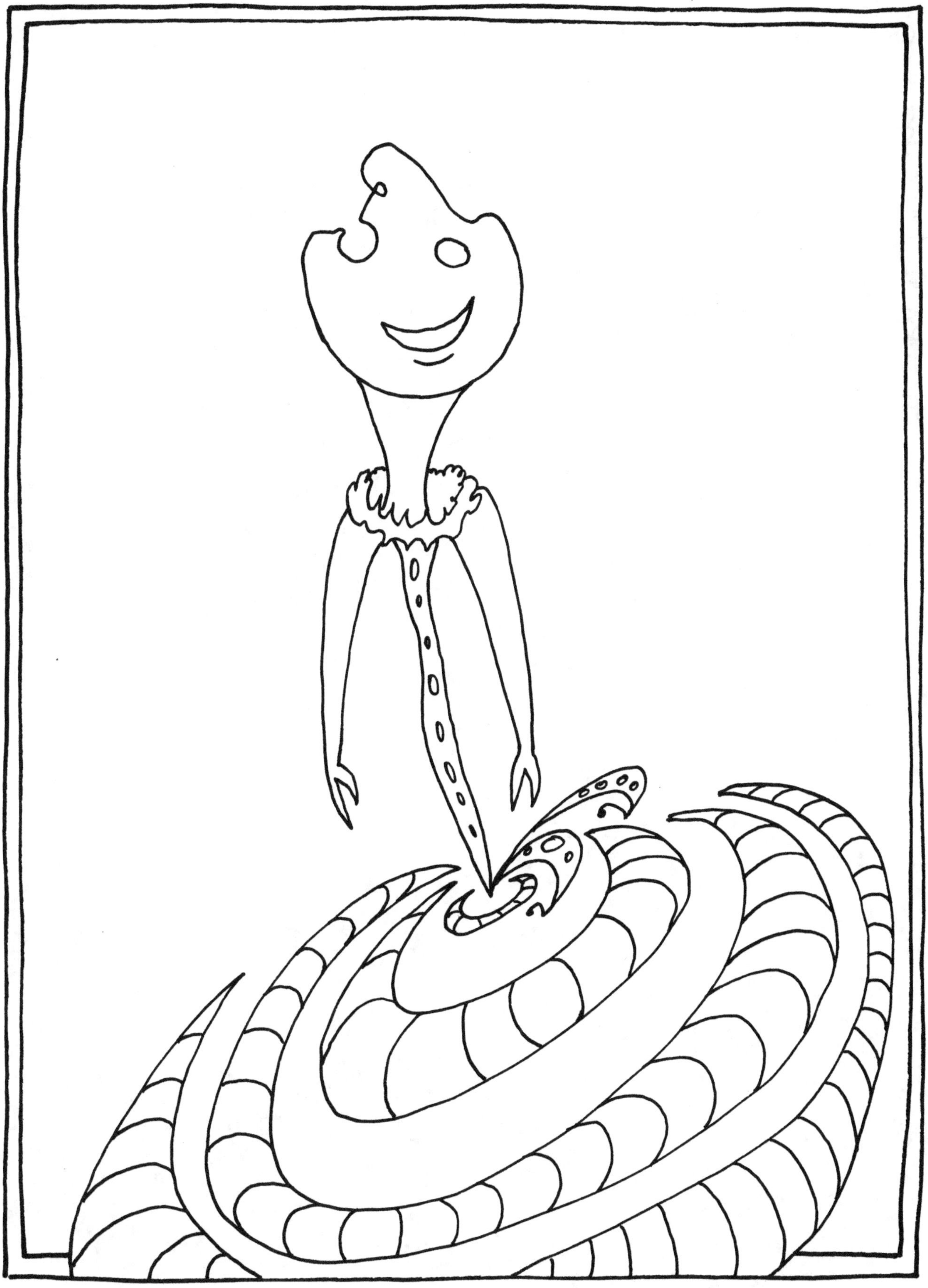

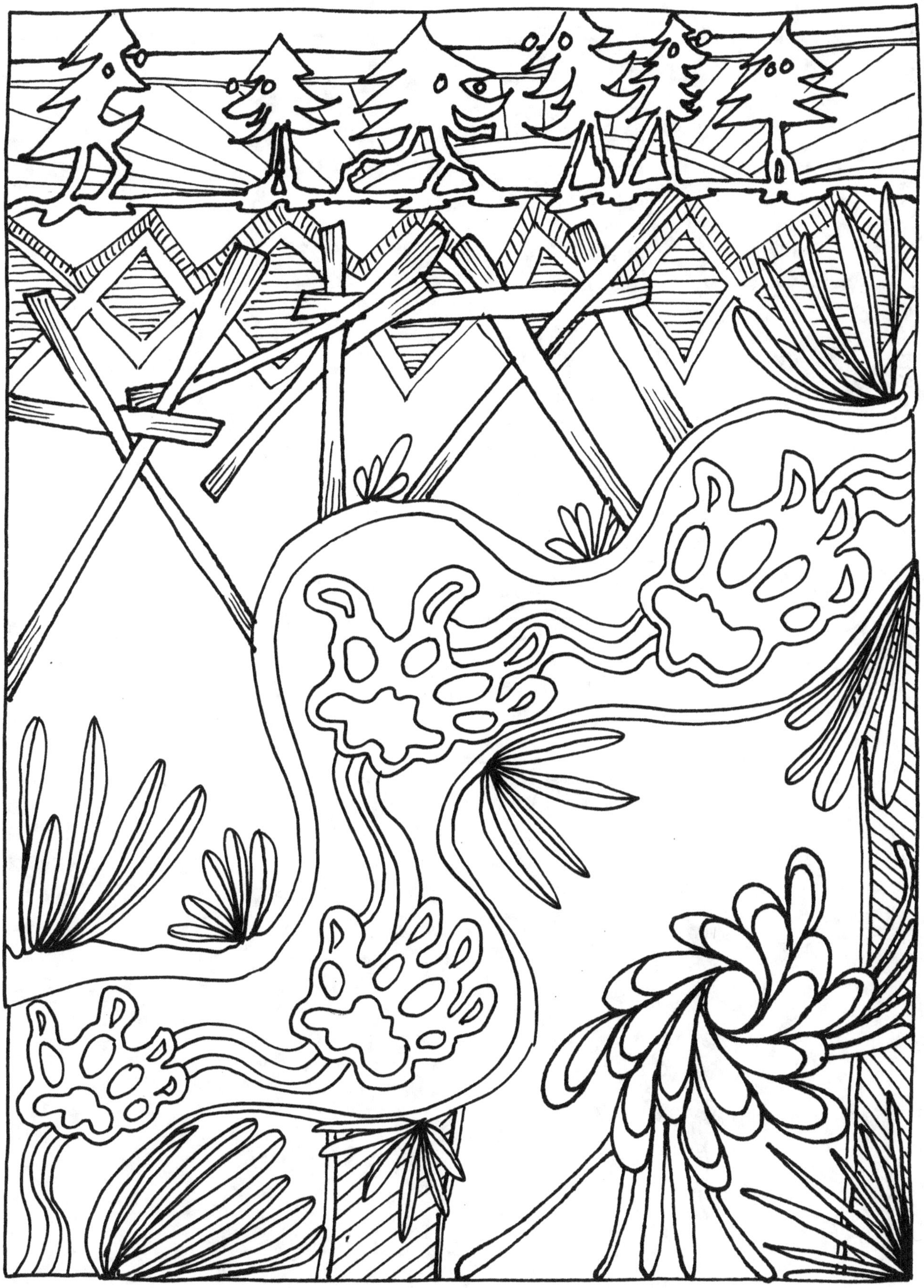

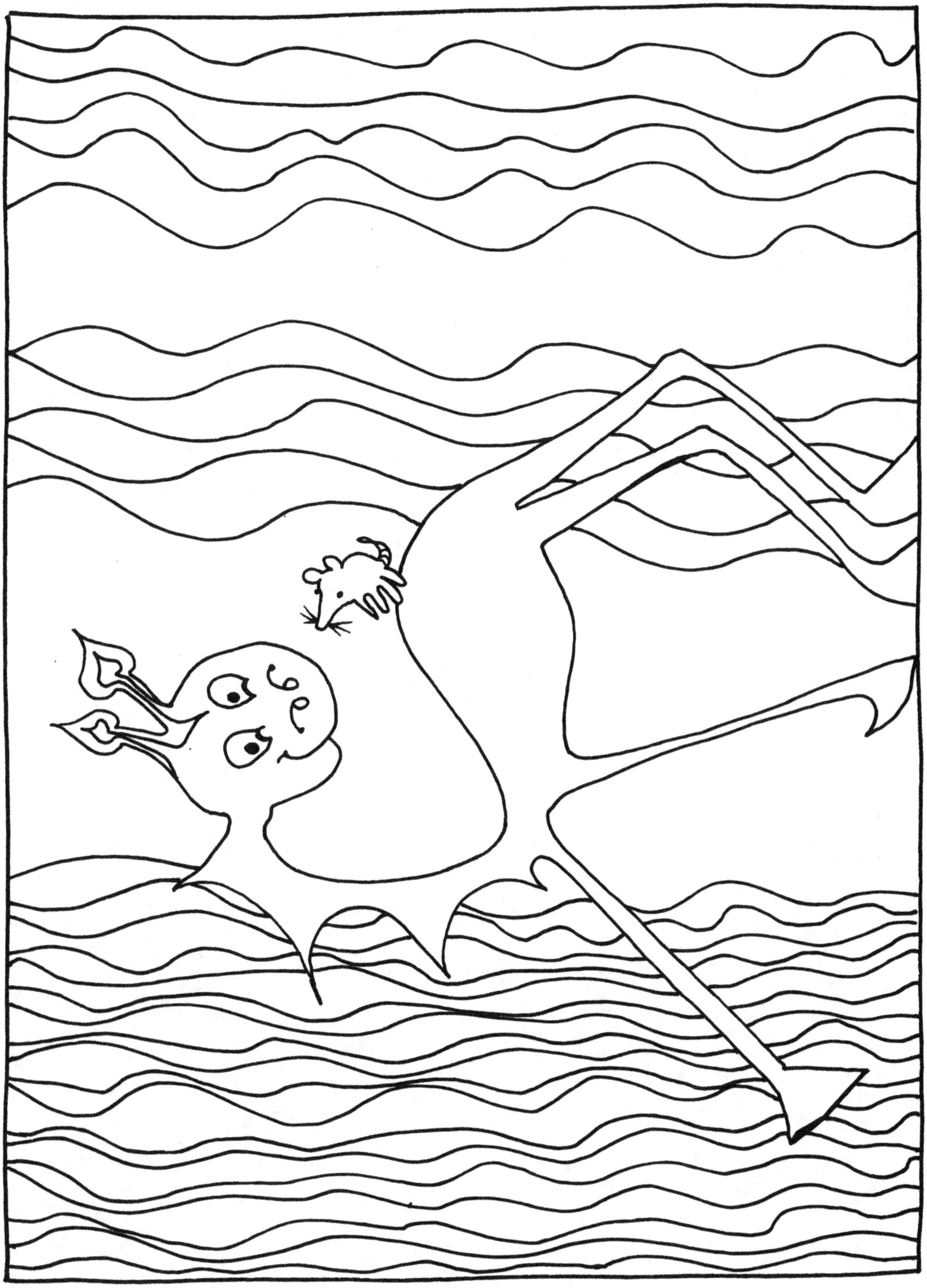

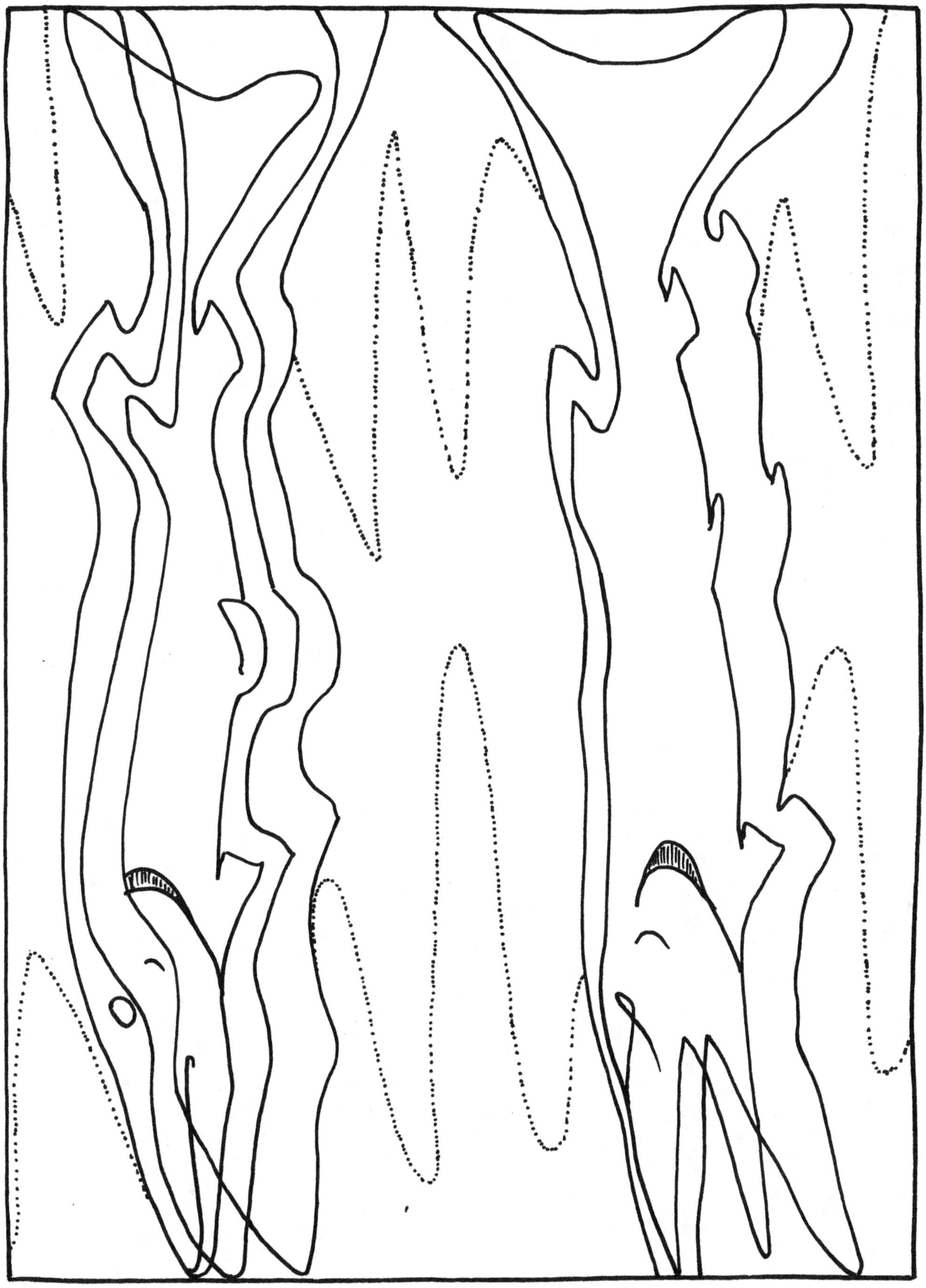

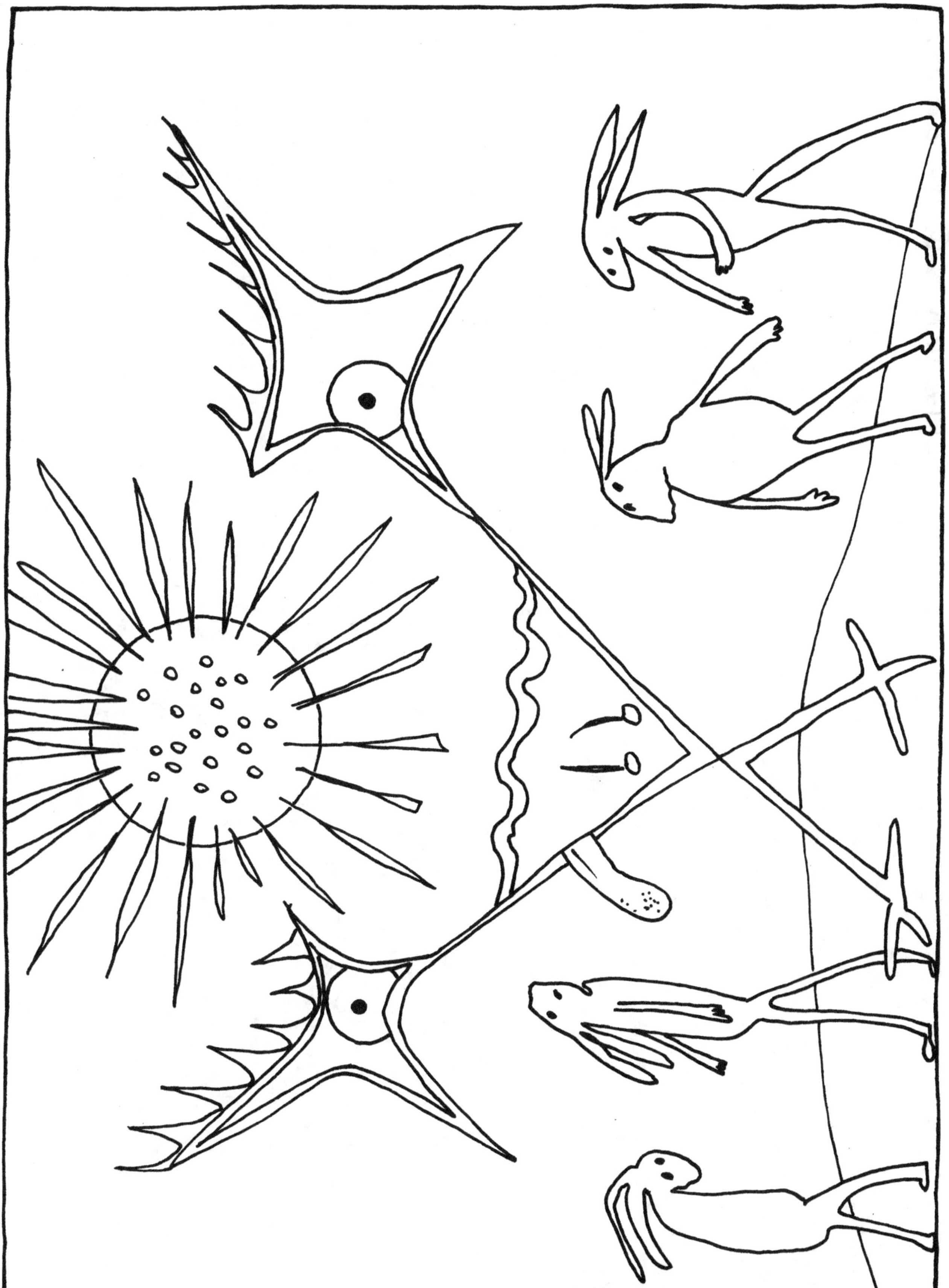

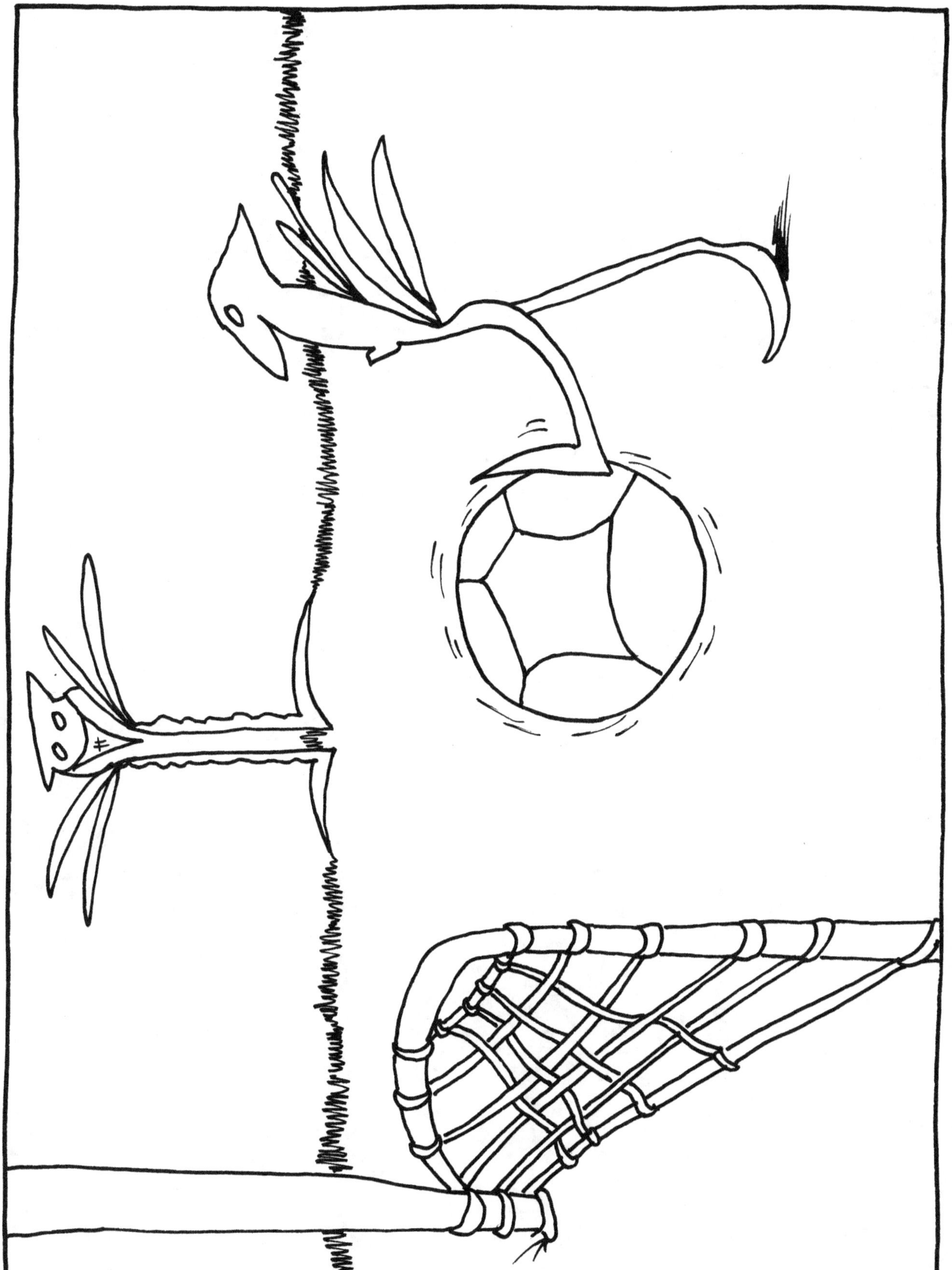

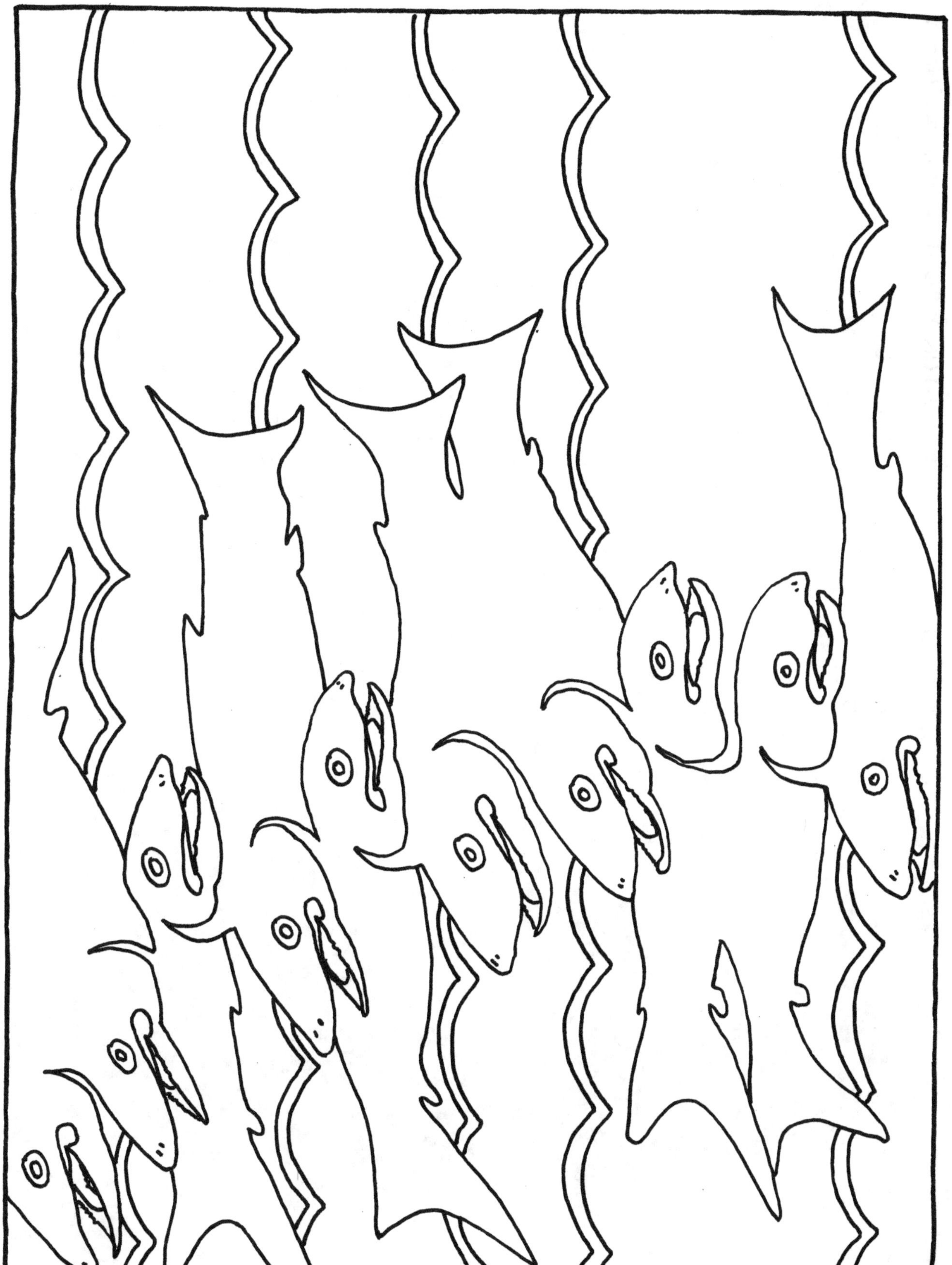

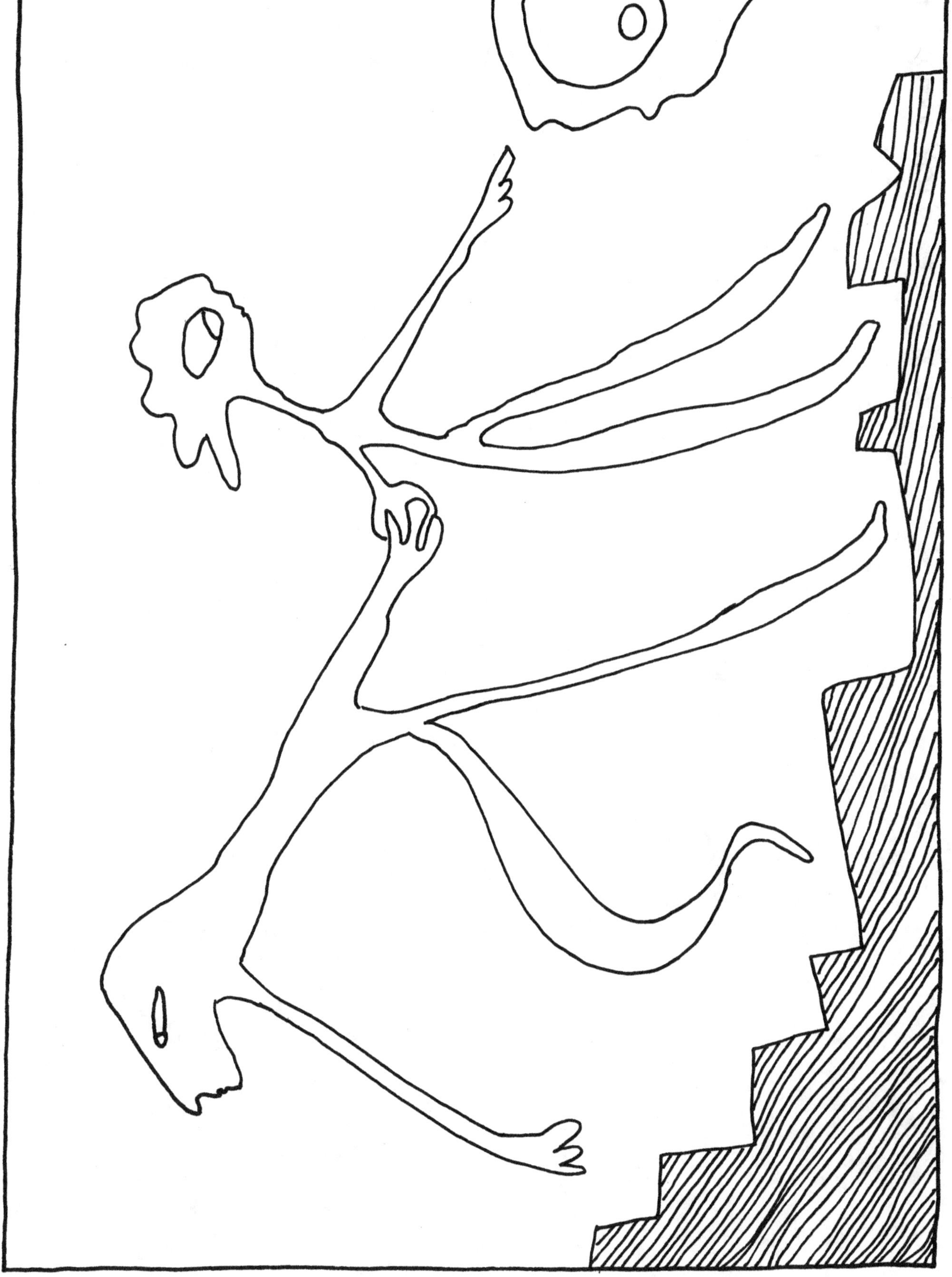

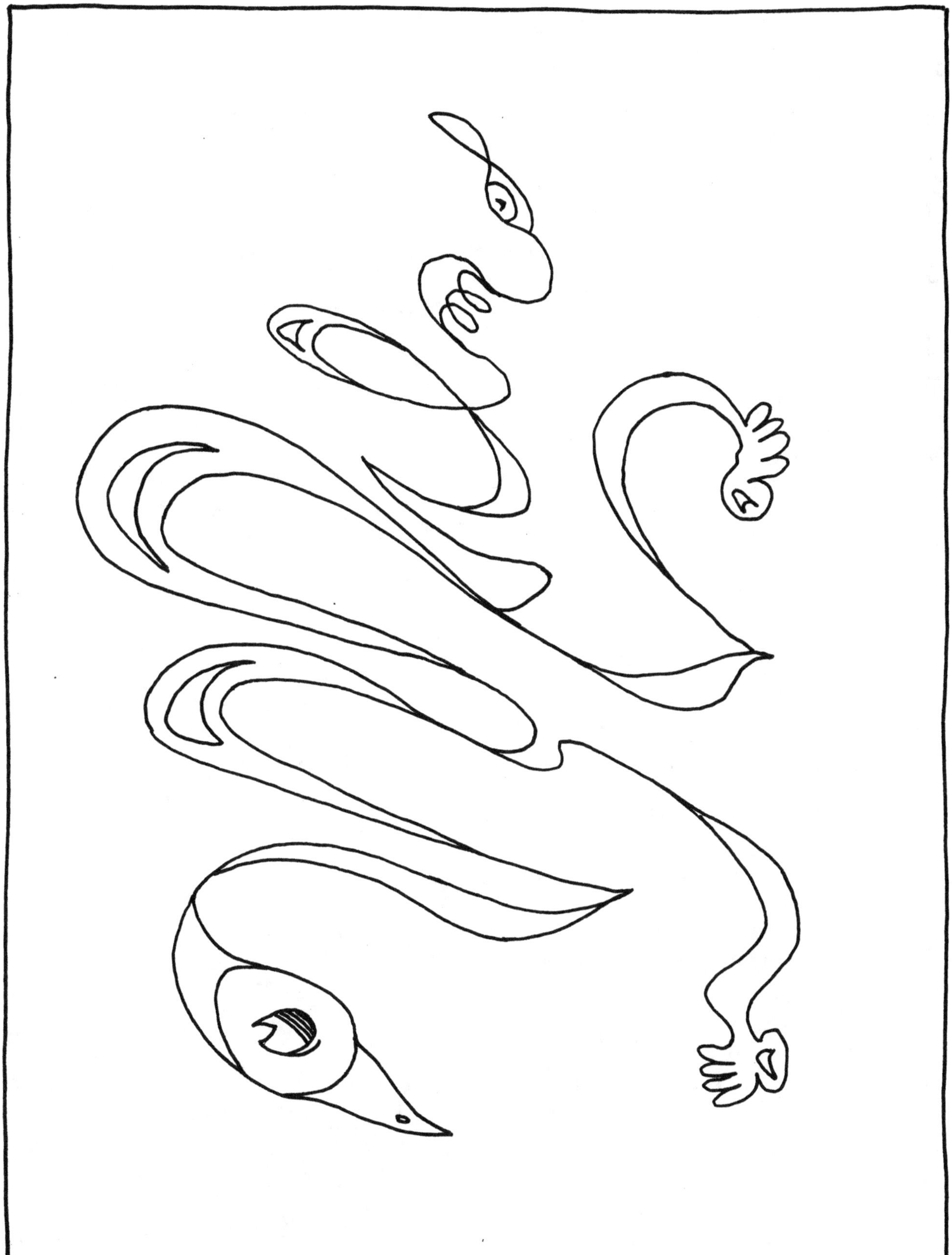

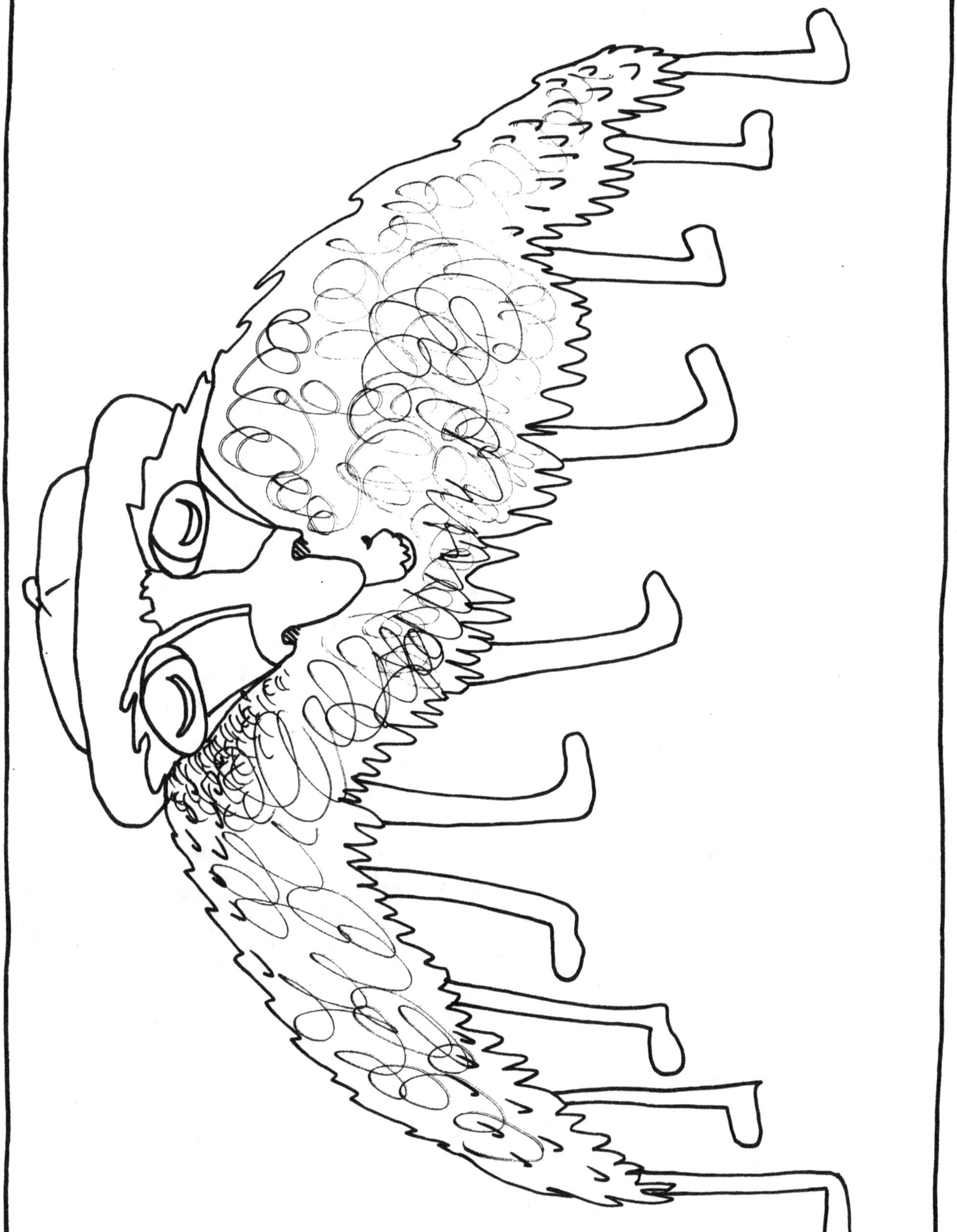

www.ingramcontent.com/pod-product-compliance
Lightning Source LLC
Chambersburg PA
CBHW081727220526
45468CB00008B/2001